HARIRI & HARIRI ARCHITECTURE

Buildings & Projects

images
Publishing

Published in Australia in 2010 by
The Images Publishing Group Pty Ltd
ABN 89 059 734 431
6 Bastow Place, Mulgrave, Victoria 3170, Australia
Tel: +61 3 9561 5544 Fax: +61 3 9561 4860
books@imagespublishing.com
www.imagespublishing.com

National Library of Australia Cataloguing-in-Publication entry:
Title: Hariri & Hariri architecture : buildings & projects.
ISBN: 9781864703405
Notes: Includes index.
Subjects: Hariri & Hariri Architecture.
                    Architects—United States.
                    Architectural firms—New York (N.Y.)
                    Architecture—United States—Pictorial works.
Dewey Number: 720.97471

Coordinating editor: Beth Browne

Production by The Graphic Image Studio Pty Ltd, Mulgrave, Australia
www.tgis.com.au

Pre-publishing services by United Graphic Pte Ltd, Singapore

Printed on 150 gsm HannoArt Matt by Everbest Printing Co. Ltd., Hong Kong/China

IMAGES has included on its website a page for special notices in relation to this and
its other publications. Please visit www.imagespublishing.com.

Every effort has been made to trace the original source of copyright material
contained in this book. The publishers would be pleased to hear from copyright
holders to rectify any errors or omissions.

The information and illustrations in this publication have been prepared and supplied
by Hariri & Hariri – Architects. While all reasonable efforts have been made to
source the required information and ensure accuracy, the publishers do not, under
any circumstances, accept responsibility for errors, omissions, and representations
express or implied.

To my mother, Behjat and father, Karim Hariri
To my sister and partner Mojgan Hariri
To my husband Bahman and my daughters Iman & Ava
To my sister Cheri, Paul, Max & Mia
To Thierry, Markus, Jenny and Bieinna
To all the remarkable women who have been my comrades
To all the remarkable men I have worked with and have learned from
To all our remarkable clients, staff, contractors, and consultants
To all my students, interns, colleagues and friends
I deeply appreciate your trust, friendship and support

FOREWORD

BY: GISUE HARIRI

We came whirling out of nothingness, scattering stars like dust,
The stars made a circle and in the middle we dance…" —Rumi

What informs our body of work? What roads brought me to where I am today? My sister (and my partner) and I were born in Iran, a land once known for being the Silk Road's wellspring of commerce and ideas. A land where great poets, such as the legendary Omar Khayam, were at once poet, mathematician, and astronomer. Once the Persian Empire, its people now fight hard to remind us that the land has a rich cultural heritage for its arts, music, literature, poetry, and sciences—all brought together and influential in its extraordinary architecture. It is a long shadow under which I find myself.

But that is not where my journey began. My earliest recollection is when, at the age of 12, I announced to my family that I was going to be an architect. While I was determined to pursue this path, I had only a youthful understanding what that meant and no realization that one day it would be a way of life, a way of seeing the world, a way of harnessing my past. My father's profession required that we live far into the desert near the oil fields. The desert became both deeply isolating and nurturing. Isolation encouraged my imagination to run wild and develop ideas that a more conventional childhood would have found odd and we often had to invent our own world, toys, and games.

The desert tends to strip everything down to the essentials without diminishing its extraordinary presence and beauty. While outwardly harsh, one familiar with its nature finds sensual lines and magnificent vistas that embolden the senses and a void that is constantly being tested and carved by the fierce wind. Where would my architecture have been without the desert?

The desert demands that its people strive for great ingenuity to survive. Buildings conform to the dictates of the harsh desert climate and the constant desert wind is harnessed with-in wind towers to cool interiors. Inside these buildings is another story. Here Iranian artists have let their well-known skills turn staid interiors into artistic masterpieces, not unlike the exquisite designs found in Persian carpets. Cities like Isfahan arose, where Iranian builders let their fantasies create their version of heaven on earth.

The desert is also a strong metaphor for women in Iran. We are isolated. We are marginalized. And, as a result, we are the most creative force in Iran today.

This mindset of continuous, holistic creativity and innovation is the hallmark of our work. Each new project is an opportunity to mine the imagination and to give our clients not only a new spatial experience but also to help them to a new way of living, where furniture, lighting, and art are all integral parts of the environment. Left to our own devices, we would like to design everything from clothing to jewelry, accessories, cars, boats, and all. To us this is all part of the same continuum.

Every summer we would visit my grandparents in Isfahan. My father's hometown is one of the few places in the world that leaves one with astonishment and awe. It is a city of amazing Persian gardens and magnificent blue-domed mosques and palaces all built by Shah Abbas the Great in the 17th century. There are pedestrian bridges like no other in the world and picturesque, organic bazaars, and a host of smaller but exquisite mosques and pleasure pavilions. Isfahan is truly the museum of Persian architecture. The tactility, materiality, and use of arts and crafts throughout our projects, regardless of scale and program, are what we carry within us from the visits to Isfahan.

When I arrived in the US in the mid-1970s to study architecture at Cornell University, I expected my sense of isolation to end but I was surprised to see very few women in the architecture program. The dismal situation extended itself to the faculty; there were no female teachers in the architectural design program. To my dismay my personal journey was to continue to be a solitary, personal, and challenging one and it became clear that it was important to find the inner voice. If architecture is ultimately the articulation and manifestation of our experiences then we should see vast differences in how each gender designs. It was however only when I began to teach that I had a chance to observe how different genders approach a given architectural project very differently. It was frustrating and disappointing to observe that women architects could never get the support they needed to develop their ideas and projects simply because they did not fit the male model of what architecture is. Problem-solving for male students is a linear, rational, and straightforward approach while women start with a tangle of multidimensional and idealistic ideas that has to go through a process of untangling, sorting, and simplifying. Most female students want to recreate their universe and multi-layered structures with a free and intuitive approach. This free approach is antithesis to the rigid, rational, linear thinking of architectural teachings in the world of established academies of architecture.

When I was a student at Cornell most professors did not want to see any curvilinear elements, human figures, landscaping, or trees in any of our drawings. They were often tagged as very "feminine" elements to have in your drawings. This attitude was a mystery to me as two beloved modernist architects we studied and became a well of inspiration—Frank Lloyd Wright and Le Corbusier—both had human figures and natural elements in most of their drawings as their whole philosophy was based on human scale and connection to nature. Such architects helped me articulate what my inner voice already knew; like the desert, the simplest things in life are the most complicated, magical, and extraordinary. What became important to us was to create memorable experiences, moments, and structures. Architecture is not about making a flamboyant form or structural gymnastics but to create environments that expand architecture's emotional possibilities to offer a wider range of human experience. It gives people the pleasure of exploring space, offering an experience of uncovering something and discovering something new. Great architecture challenges our perception of life and living and finds an alternative mode of seeing and acting upon the landscape. Architecture is more than the construction of buildings; it is where our dreams transcend realities of life. It is a commitment that will carry you to places you had neither dreamed of nor knew even existed before you began.

Architecture cannot be defined as one thing, style, philosophy, or "ism." It is the amalgamation of many things, which at its best helps us define who we are today and who we might be tomorrow. It's the means of comprehending and encountering the invisible, where beauty, sensuality, functionality, technology and philosophy connect the body and mind.

MIXED USE

SALZBURG RESIDENTIAL COMPLEX

2006–2012

CLIENT: ERNST SCHOLDAN/ASSET ONE IMMOBILIENENTWICKLUNGS AG
LOCATION: SALZBURG, AUSTRIA
TOTAL AREA: 5.1 ACRES
SITE: 3.3 ACRES
AREA OF CONSTRUCTION: 151,136 SQUARE FEET ABOVE GRADE; 247,419 SQUARE FEET TOTAL
PROGRAM: 80 LUXURY APARTMENTS; RESTAURANT; SPA; ART GALLERY;
HOUSE OF ARCHITECTURE AND UNDERGROUND PARKING GARAGE
PROJECTED COST: US $80 MILLION
STATUS: UNDER CONSTRUCTION
GROUND BREAKING: SEPTEMBER 2007
PROJECTED COMPLETION DATE: 2012

Inspired by the defining natural elements of the City of Salzburg, this proposal takes form. The master plan abstractly follows the city plan and becomes a microcosm of the city of Salzburg, with its distinctive mountains and the Salzach River flowing through.

To create a dialogue and a personal, meditative experience a narrow creek was cut at the edge of the rock wall, which guides and invites the public through the site. Just like the Salzach River, it creates a new boundary, provides movement, and extends nature into the site. An old public path is incorporated in this sequence. Water travels from the highest elevation on the site through a series of waterfalls, collecting melted snow, icicles, and rocks. This pedestrian path is carefully designed to allow the public to enjoy the natural beauty of the forest and the rock face without disturbing residents' privacy. The water canal provides a place for exhibiting outdoor water sculptures, a spiritual space for meditation, and spa facilities for the proposed wellness center.

Architecturally, this project simulates the rock formation, deposits, and random composition of a quarry site where pieces of rocks are chiseled from the mountain and then cut into smaller pieces and stacked up in a random fashion. Each block then becomes a container, a wrapping enclosure of smaller blocks or apartments within, allowing each living unit to be unique with magnificent views. With this approach, the mountain becomes a "generator" rather than a "backdrop." The proposed buildings are set back from the rock face. They hover over their bases just enough to create a tension, from where one could almost reach out and touch the rock.

Eighty luxury residences will occupy the six new structures on the site, none of which reach more that eight stories in height. The program also includes exhibition space for the House of Architecture, a gallery and lecture space in the old brewery's underground vaults.

Covering the subterranean facility will be a public green space punctured by sculptural skylights jutting from the ground. A restaurant has been proposed at a location where people will be able to enjoy the rock. In a way, the whole complex is designed around the experiential qualities of the site. Our expectation is that, like music, this place will resonate in its visitors' memories long after they have left.

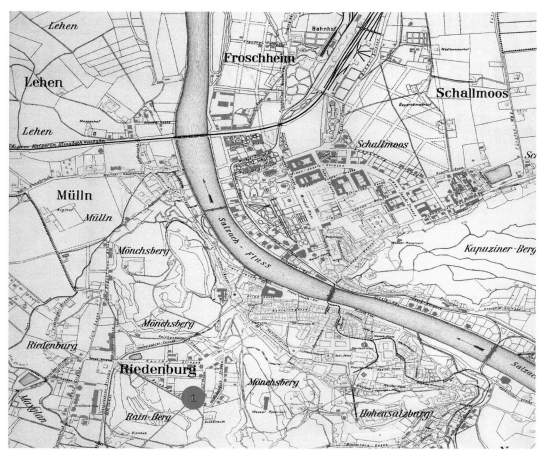

EXPERIENCE:

Salzach River

City textures

Typical buildings with their back to the rock

Existing rockface on the edge of the site

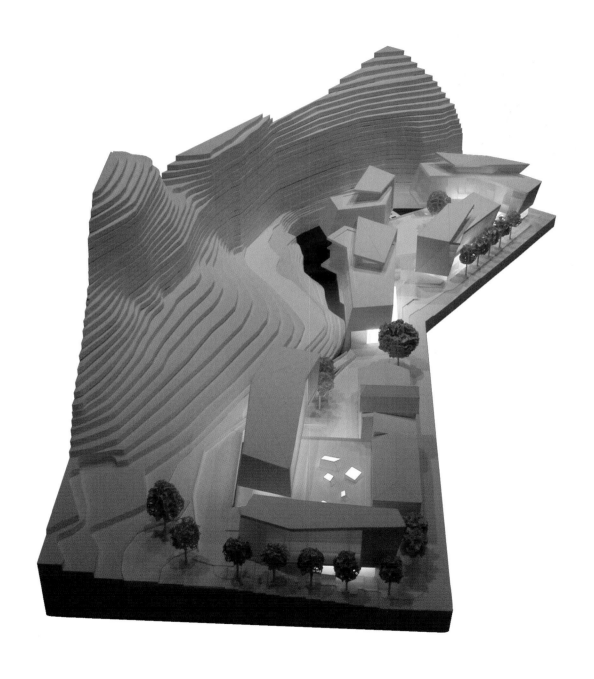

1 EXISTING ROCK FACE
2 PROPOSED WATER CANAL
3 COURTYARD
4 PROPOSED NEW BUILDINGS A–G
5 ROOF TERRACE OVER EXISTING VAULTS
6 ENTRY TO PUBLIC PATH

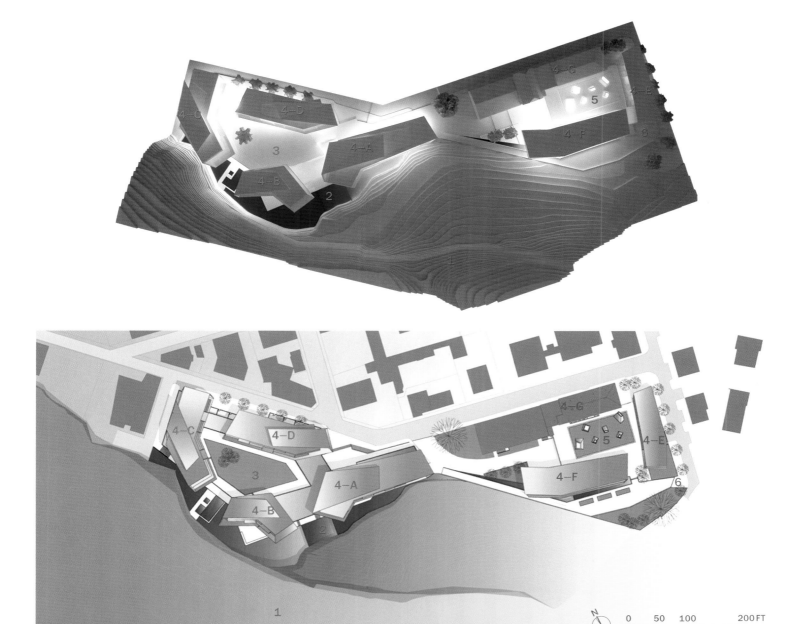

PROPOSED PLAN: SECTION OF BUILDING BLOCK B
VIEW OF BUILDINGS C, B & A

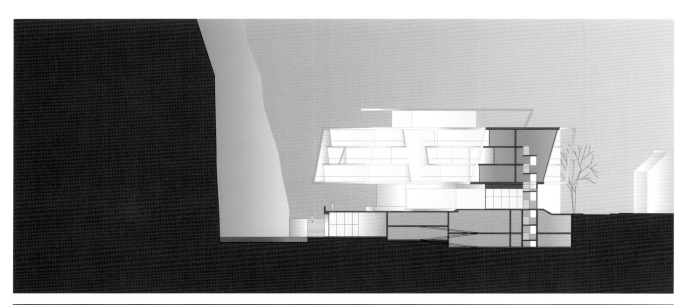

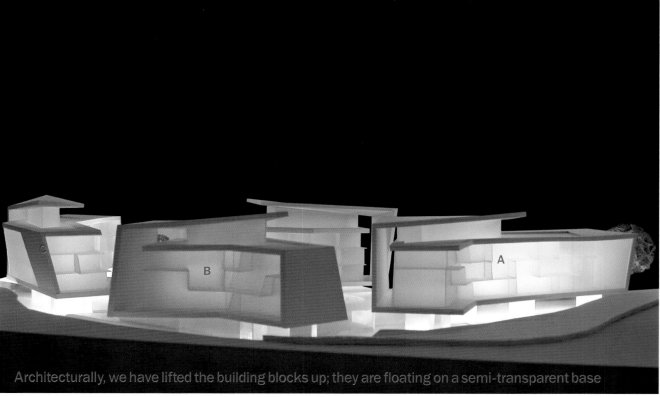

Architecturally, we have lifted the building blocks up; they are floating on a semi-transparent base

PROPOSED PLAN: PLANS OF BUILDING BLOCK A

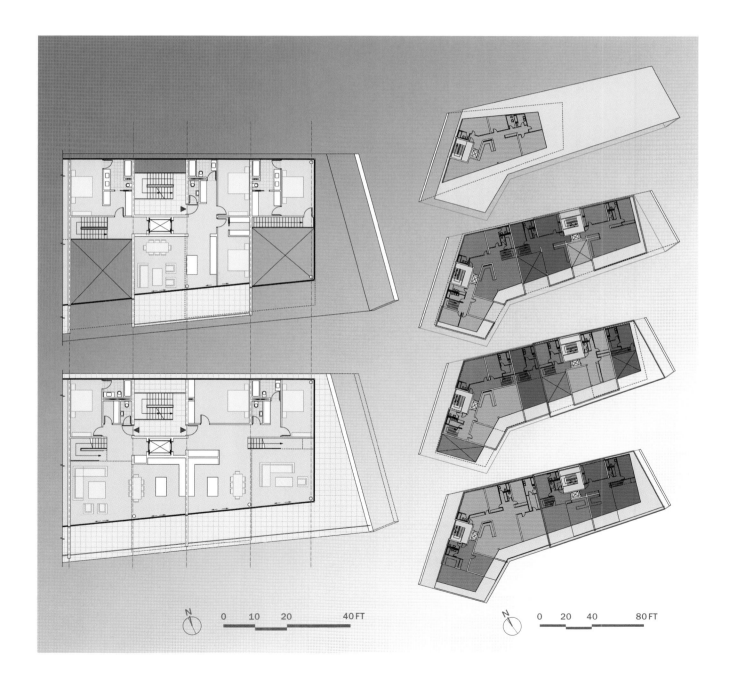

N   0   10   20   40 FT

N   0   20   40   80 FT

Living room with waterfall view

Living room with city view

Penthouse terrace with city view

Typical kitchen with rock face view

Spa and wellness center with view of Building B

Just like the Salzach River, this water canal creates a new boundary, provides movement, and extends nature into the site

The proposed buildings are set back from the rock face. They hover over their bases just enough to create a tension, from where one could almost reach out and touch the rock.

Building F

Street view of whole complex

1. Interior courtyard between Buildings C and D
2. Building B and restaurant
3. Meeting in Salzburg with city officials
4. Ground breaking (right to left): developer, architects, mayor and building officials
5. Project under construction

THE HIGH LINE COMMUNITY

2003–2012

LOCATION: **NEW YORK CITY, NEW YORK, USA**
SITE: **EXISTING ELEVATED RAILROAD ON 10TH AVENUE
BETWEEN 12TH AND 34TH STREETS**
PROGRAM: **MIXED-USE TOWERS (PUBLIC/PRIVATE HYBRIDS)**
STATUS: **COMPETITION HONORABLE MENTION AND SELECTED ENTRY FOR EXHIBITION
AT GRAND CENTRAL STATION**
PROJECTED COMPLETION DATE: **2012**

The High Line (Elevated Railway between Gansevoort and 34th Street in the Chelsea area of New York City) is a distinctive part of New York's history and should be embraced by the urban fabric of the city. Completed in 1933, the High Line was intended to be a vital component of a modern, multilevel New York. New development should expand upon this historic identity and take advantage of its unique architectural possibilities.

In this proposal, we envision a community of mixed-use towers (public/private hybrids) to be built over the High Line. These towers, and the openings through which pedestrians will move, conceptually assimilate the historic passage and recall the movement of trains through buildings.

These towers will have approximately 100 feet or 10 stories of cultural, commercial, and public space at their base where the High Line goes through, with residential units above.

The mixed-use towers could house Olympic athletes and offer meeting halls, auditoriums, cafeterias, physical training and fitness centers, internet and media lounges, souvenir shops, and spacious outdoor covered areas for athletes to interact in, allowing New York to compete for hosting the Olympic Games.

To facilitate this development, we propose an Olympic-size stadium to be built at the 30th Street Rail Yards. The base of the stadium will offer two levels of retail space, the upper of which will be adjacent to and accessed from the High Line. The upper level will also provide a large public roof garden. This development will mark one end of the High Line and bring vital activity to the High Line as a new, elevated pedestrian walkway.

Finally, the High Line Community will be an essential part of 21st-century New York, vertical and dense, interwoven into the existing urban fabric, "a city within a city." It will offer variety of required residential, cultural, sports, commercial, and public spaces as a unified design to New York City. The High Line will be paved with translucent panels lit from beneath, providing a continuous horizontal glow. This elevated passageway will take visitors on an exuberant journey through the neighborhood, experiencing architecture of extruded concrete public spaces reflecting the activities of the 21st century and celebrating the spirit of New York in the new millennium.

SITE/DIAGRAM:

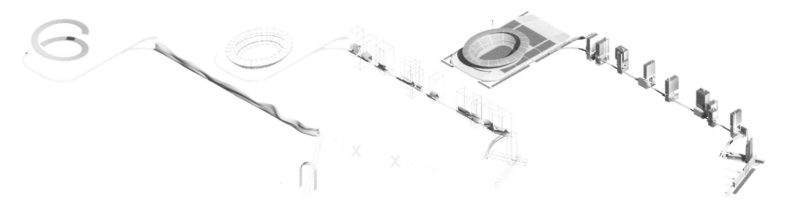

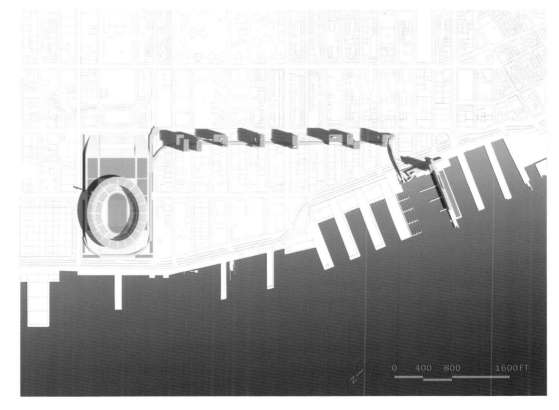

0   400   800   1600 FT

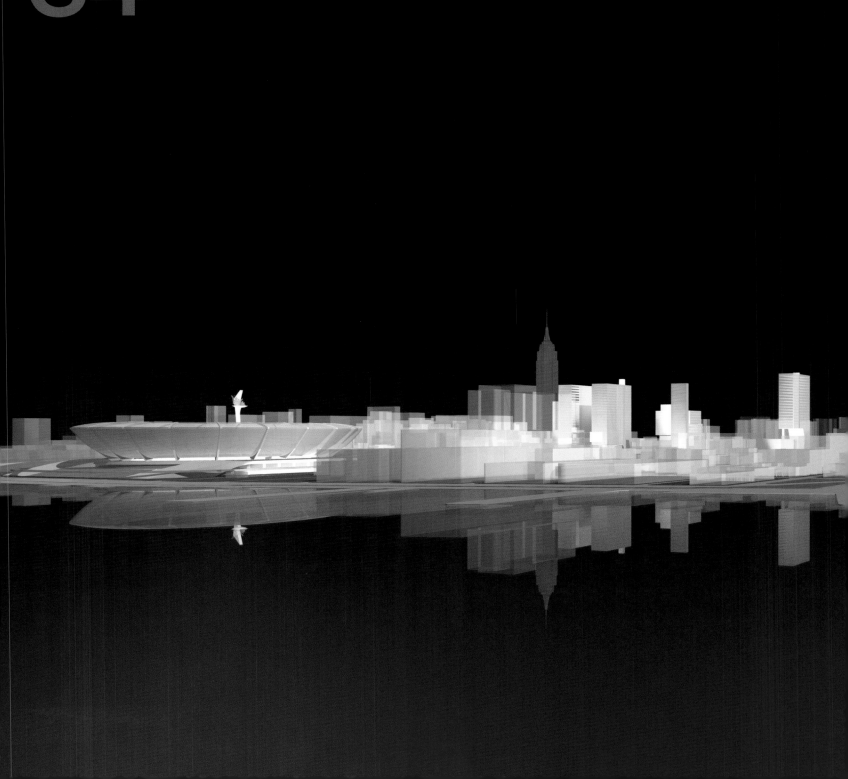

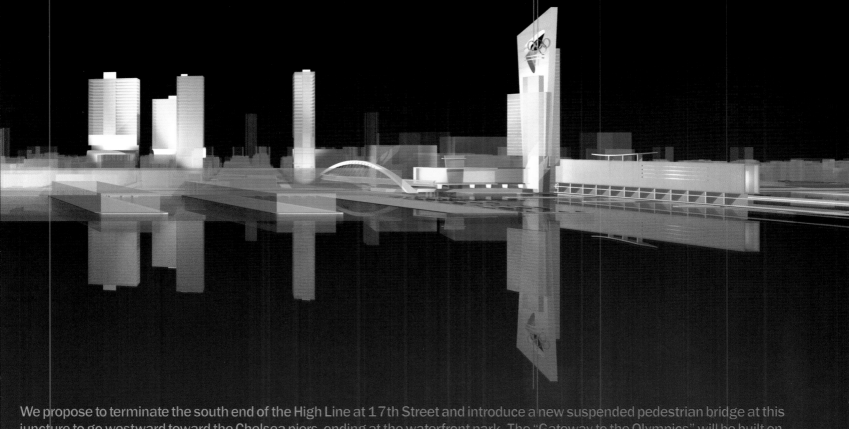

We propose to terminate the south end of the High Line at 17th Street and introduce a new suspended pedestrian bridge at this juncture to go westward toward the Chelsea piers, ending at the waterfront park. The "Gateway to the Olympics" will be built on this location, at Pier 57, and will commemorate the Olympic Games of 2012.

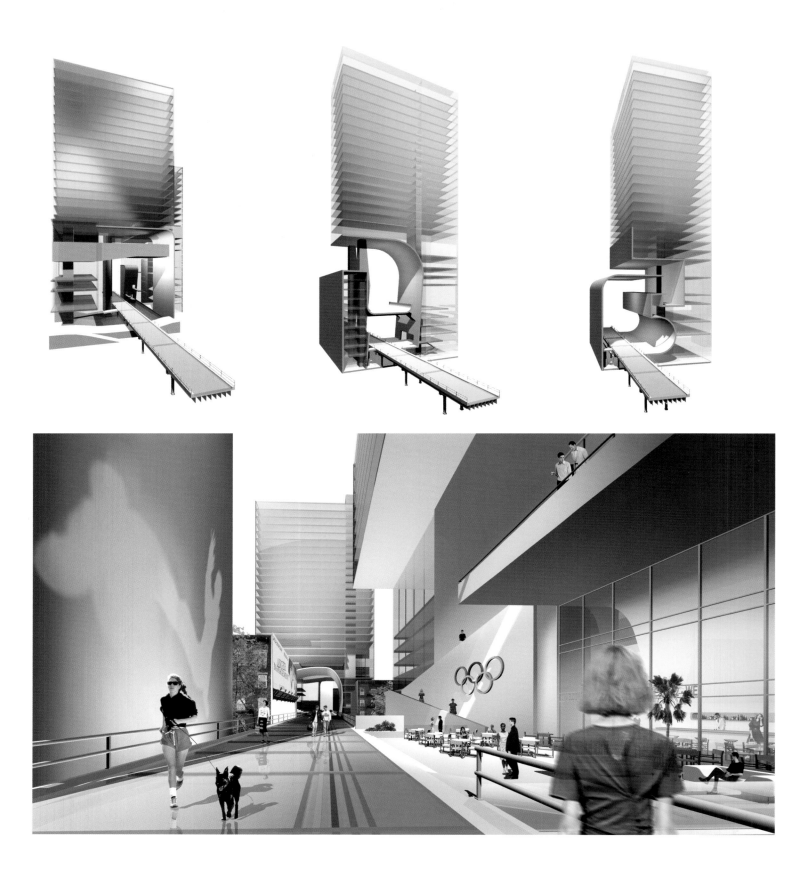

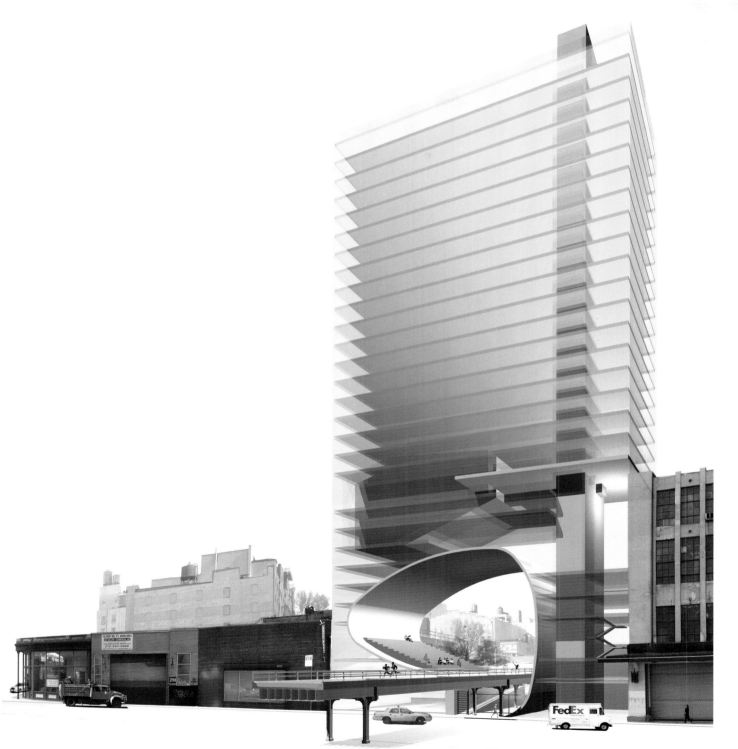

The mixed-use towers between 17th and 30th Streets offer housing for Olympic athletes and meeting halls, auditoriums, cafeterias, physical training, and fitness centers. Internet and media lounges, souvenir shops, and spacious covered outdoor areas for athletes to interact in are integrated throughout the project.

CANADIAN COPTIC VILLAGE

2003–2011

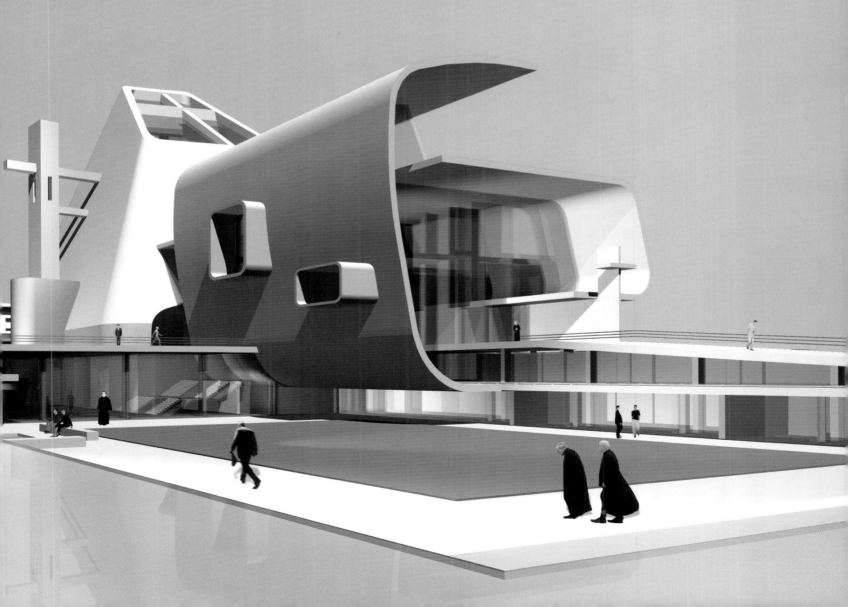

LOCATION: **CITY OF MARKHAM (NORTH OF TORONTO), ONTARIO, CANADA**
TOTAL AREA: **12 ACRES**
PROGRAM: **2,500-SEAT CATHEDRAL, 2,000-SEAT CHURCH, COMMUNITY CENTER, DAYCARE CENTER, RETIREMENT HOME, SCHOOL, MUSEUM, OFFICE BUILDING, PARKING**
ESTIMATED COST: **US $200 MILLION**
STATUS: **COMPETITION FINALIST**
PROJECTED COMPLETION DATE: **2011**

Following the ideology of monasticism and monastic architecture, which was instrumental in the formation of the Coptic church, this proposed 21st-century Coptic Center will be composed of a large central space enclosed by an L-shaped group of buildings. The buildings will frame a large central plaza or courtyard exhibiting the "jewels" of the project—the cathedral and the church. These holy spaces are designed as sculptural objects within the plaza and are located on Steeles Avenue. A 13-foot-high plinth/plaza forms the lowest part of the site. This plinth or base holding the cathedral and the church constitutes the first phase of this proposal. The base will include three levels of underground parking as well.

The center begins with the spiritual elements of the program. Both buildings will be oriented east–west according to the tradition of Coptic orthodox churches, utilizing a square plan with a large dome in the shape of a pyramid and a large angled skylight, bringing light and identity to the center, and celebrating the origin of the Egyptian–Coptic culture. These holy spaces symbolize the Lord's divinity and humanity, and are united by the plinth/plaza. The entrance to the cathedral is via a ramp through an entry in the form of two hands holding the cross. We have retained the traditional sequence of narthex, nave, and deacons' platform with three altars at the end to organize the cathedral and church plans. However, the spirit of the 21st century is expressed in this proposal through transparency and the design of its nave, offering openness and freedom throughout the center and to the surrounding community. The church's main entrance is from the sunken plaza accessed through a series of steps from the drop-off area. It is similar in form to the cathedral but is smaller in dimensions.

1 COMMUNITY CENTER
2 PRIVATE SCHOOL
3 DAYCARE
4 SENIORS' APARTMENT BUILDING
5 RETIREMENT/NURSING HOME
6 CHURCH
7 BISHOP RESIDENCY
8 MUSEUM
9 CATHEDRAL
10 SUNDAY SCHOOL
11 OFFICE BUILDING

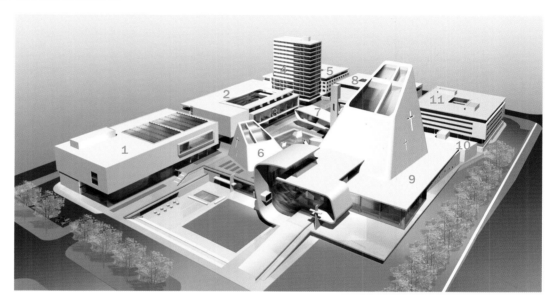

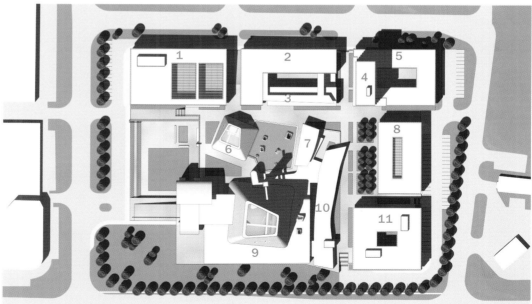

N   0   50 100   200 FT

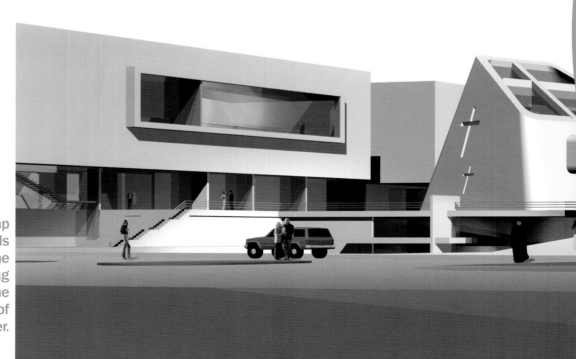

The entrance to the cathedral is via a ramp through an entry in the form of two hands holding the cross. The main cross of the cathedral, lit from within and hovering 150 feet above the ground, will be the most visible, signifying the essence of this Coptic Center.

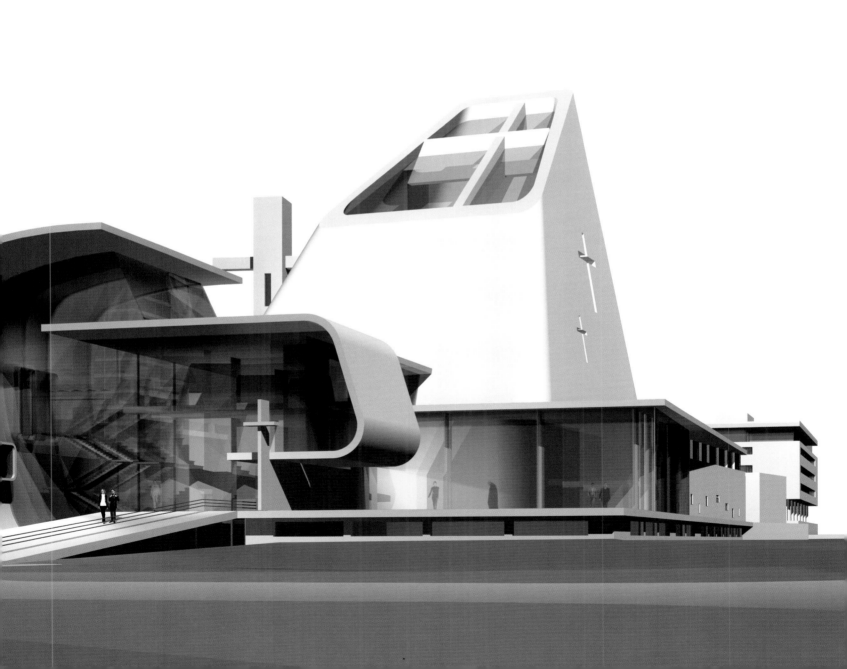

A large reflecting pool of water located between the cathedral and the church has seven sculptural light scoops bringing light down into the chapels, the church's altars, and the shared spaces below. This reflecting pool of water not only brings light to these spaces, it also acts as an outdoor holy space for meditation and prayer at the heart of this center.

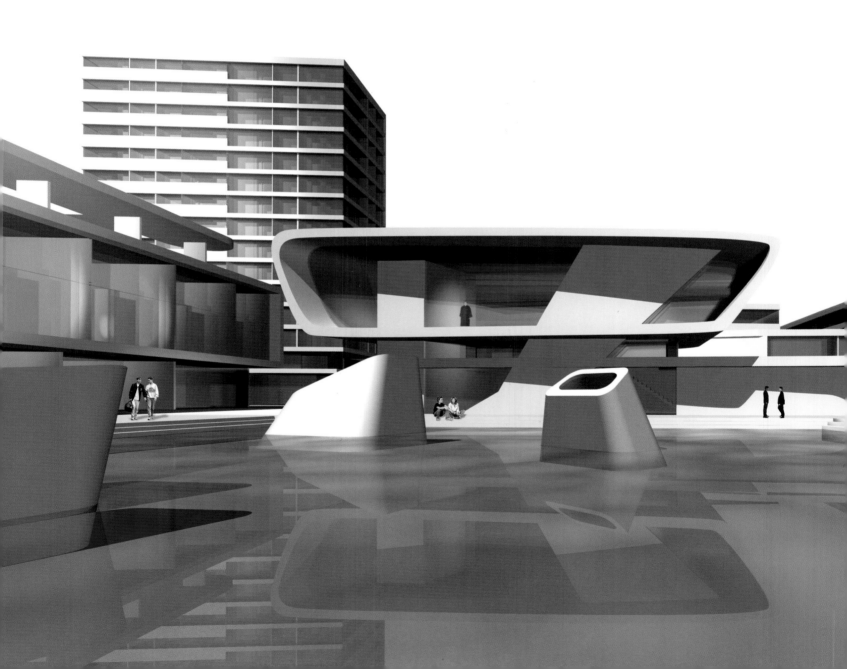

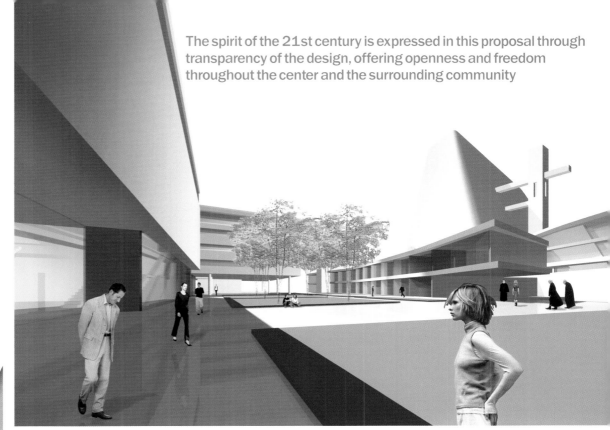

The spirit of the 21st century is expressed in this proposal through transparency of the design, offering openness and freedom throughout the center and the surrounding community

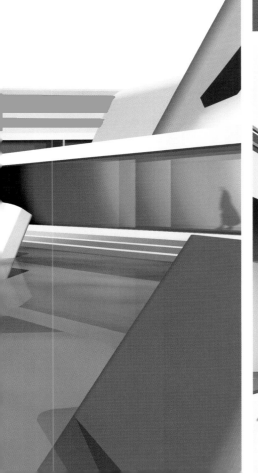

The sunken plaza will serve as an outdoor congregation area and a forecourt to both the cathedral and the church

DALLAS

LOFT BUILDING

2006–2010

CLIENT: **BILLINGSLEY DEVELOPMENT COMPANY**
LANDSCAPE: **MESA DESIGN GROUP**
LOCATION: **ARTS PLAZA, DALLAS, TEXAS, USA**
SITE: **DALLAS CULTURAL CENTER, TWO ARTS PLAZA DEVELOPMENT**
TOTAL AREA: **50,000 SQUARE FEET**
PROGRAM: **16 URBAN LOFTS**
PROJECTED COST: **US $15 MILLION**
STATUS: **CONSTRUCTION DOCUMENT PHASE**
PROJECTED COMPLETION DATE: **2010**

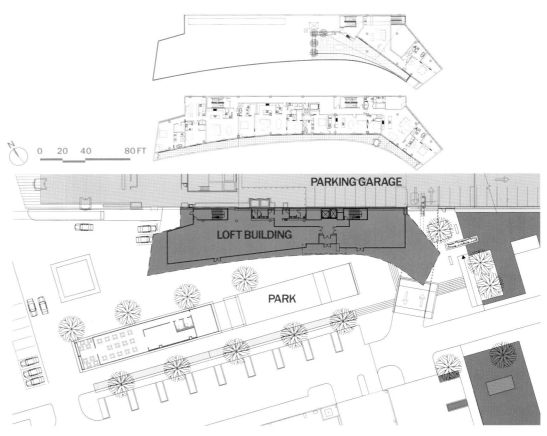

This sculptural, high-end, luxury residential building is being developed as part of the prestigious mixed-use Two Arts Plaza project in the heart of Dallas's cultural center.

It is located on a challenging sliver of land adjacent to a mixed-use high-rise building with a triangular urban park in the front. This structure not only has to act as a work of "Art in the Park" but it also has to disguise the undesirable concrete wall of the seven-story parking garage behind.

Inspired by the neighborhood's art and cultural facilities, its urban gardens, and pedestrian nature, the Loft Building as a whole takes the form of a sculpture in the park. It is 320 feet long, 30 feet deep, and 70 feet high.

This sculptural building conceals the undesirable concrete wall of the parking structure behind, but it peels away and frees itself from the surrounding rigid and formal structures, with a gentle curve embracing the small park space in the front. The main façade is glass and stucco with a large window, or frame, creating an indoor/outdoor terrace space for each loft.

This six-story structure has 16 lofts, a duplex penthouse, and commercial/retail spaces on the ground level. It offers a new kind of urban living, uncommon in Dallas, as most people live in either high-rise condominiums or single-family homes. Urban loft living began in American cities when people started moving to suburbs and artists began to move in and occupy abandoned manufacturing and industrial buildings in search of larger spaces at lower prices. It is all about openness, light, and space.

The lobby and the top five floors of residential condominiums in the high-rise building next to the Loft Building were also designed by Hariri & Hariri as part of the same complex.

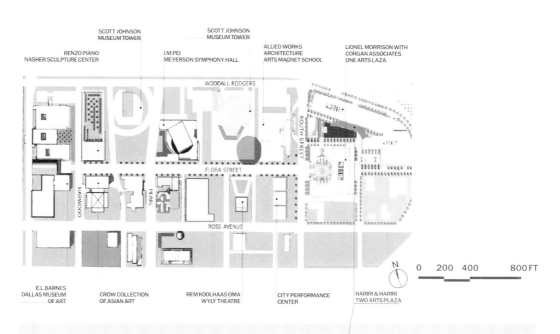

SCOTT JOHNSON
MUSEUM TOWER

SCOTT JOHNSON
MUSEUM TOWER

ALLIED WORKS
ARCHITECTURE
ARTS MAGNET SCHOOL

LIONEL MORRISON WITH
CORGAN ASSOCIATES
ONE ARTS LAZA

RENZO PIANO
NASHER SCULPTURE CENTER

I.M.PEI
MEYERSON SYMPHONY HALL

WOODALL RODGERS

ROUTH STREET

FLORA STREET

HARWOOD

PEARL

ROSS AVENUE

N

0   200 400   800 FT

E.L.BARNES
DALLAS MUSEUM
OF ART

CROW COLLECTION
OF ASIAN ART

REM KOOLHAAS OMA
WYLY THEATRE

CITY PERFORMANCE
CENTER

HARIRI & HARIRI
TWO ARTS PLAZA

Lobby of Loft Building

The architecture offers a new kind
of urban living uncommon in Dallas

Following the sculptural exterior of the building and continuation of the same fluid design concept inside, the lobby offers continuous space, folded planes, lighting, and details rare in speculative residential architecture

A composition of materials in stone, glass and mosaic tiles, fabric, and wood bring scale, tactility, and warmth to the lobby, waiting area, and all the apartment interiors

Lofts with fireplace, folding wall, and lighting details

Rooftop lounge

A lounge with indoor/outdoor pool and spa facilities on the 22nd floor completes the rooftop of this livable, modern project

SOUTH STREET TOWER

2007

LOCATION: NEW YORK CITY, NEW YORK, USA
SITE: 8,216 SQUARE FEET
TOTAL AREA: 271,200 SQUARE FEET
PROGRAM: THE 51-STORY TOWER CONTAINS 27 FLOORS OF LUXURY RESIDENTIAL UNITS,
23 FLOORS OF OFFICE SPACE, SKY SPA WITH FITNESS CENTER AND
SWIMMING POOL, LANDSCAPED TERRACE, PARKING FACILITIES, AND GROUND
FLOOR COMMERCIAL AND RESIDENTIAL LOBBIES ALONGSIDE RETAIL SPACE
STATUS: DESIGN PHASE

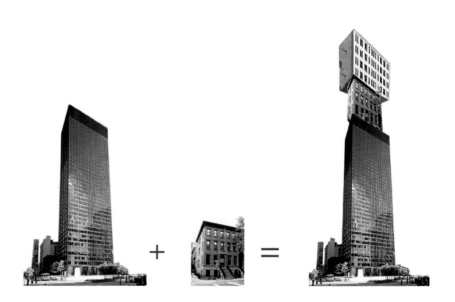

Inspired by New York City's architecture of office towers and residential town houses, this mixed-use tower takes form. Conceptually, this project is a fusion of two iconic types offering a new and original "typological hybrid" with a monolithic base containing the commercial office spaces transforming into shifting blocks and smaller residential units on top.

The ratio between the size of the lot and the height of the tower results in a slender, sliver-like mass. The concept of "typological hybrid" has allowed us to have a simple, elegant tower that relates contextually to the city yet is distinct and iconic in form and proportion. The articulation of the residential blocks on top not only allows for terraces and different apartment types, it also provides spectacular views with shifting perspectives and creates a dynamic landmark that is recognizable from everywhere. This 51-story mixed-use tower accommodates 23 floors of commercial/office space and 27 floors of residential condominiums.

CONCEPT/MODEL: Complementing the hybrid nature of the architecture, a hybrid of technologies creates an environmentally green building. Solar PV panels integrated in the skin of the building in combination with wind turbines on the roof will generate electricity and reduce energy costs. Geothermal wells will serve as a partial source for heating and cooling and reduce boiler size requirements.

The building skin is envisioned as a glass curtain wall with integrated photovoltaic panels. The PV panels will be made of thin film solar modules laminated between two layers of glass. They will run vertically in narrow strips along the façade of the commercial portion of the tower and generate electricity from the sun's rays, providing energy savings.

Structurally the tower is also a hybrid of steel to the top of the commercial levels and flat slab concrete for the residential levels.

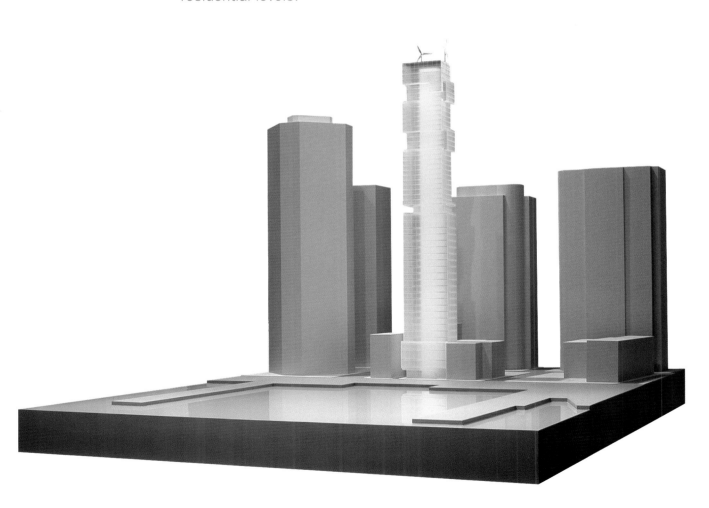

The narrow strips turn into LED lighting at the mechanical levels, and into clear operable windows at the residential levels.

A 15- by 45-foot swimming pool in a double-story space surrounded by glass and a wraparound outdoor terrace is located on the 24th floor

WTC WEEPING TOWERS

2002

LOCATION: NEW YORK CITY, NEW YORK, USA
SITE: GROUND ZERO
PROGRAM: 11 MIXED-USE, COMMERCIAL/RETAIL, CULTURAL TOWERS
APPROXIMATELY 80-100 STORIES HIGH
STATUS: DESIGN IDEA EXHIBITED AT MAX PROTETCH GALLERY, NATIONAL BUILDING MUSEUM
AND VENICE BIENNALE

At times of horrific and outrageous disasters, great cities have not only rebuilt their collapsed structures but also have become laboratories and testing grounds for the development of new architecture and urbanism. Due to digital technology and electronic communication, financial industries no longer need to be situated on top of one another and have been diversifying away from downtown for a decade now. As a result most of the office space lost on September 11 is no longer needed.

We propose an evolving structure composed of 11 towers approximately 80–100 stories high. These towers symbolically represent the heroic scale of the Twin Towers but only serve as vertical circulation, mechanical, electrical, and digital cores for the floors and programs to come. These 11 cores will act as an infrastructure where the new occupants will bring their prefabricated buildings and structures via ships and trucks, plugging into the structural scaffold. The exterior of the towers will be wrapped in smart skins where information and data can be displayed both to the occupants inside and visitors on the outside. The skin would also be equipped with a sprinkler system and a device detecting objects approaching the building.

In contrast to the orthogonal towers there will be a number of freeform buildings, blurring the boundaries of architectural building types. These structures would be very large, reaching between the towers and housing programs like theaters, a cultural museum, sky plazas, and sport facilities, among others. We envision the new state-of-the-art New York Stock Exchange to be housed at one of these buildings at the heart of the complex to signify, in a way visible to the entire city, the strength of the world's financial capital.

As a memorial we reject a sentimental physical memorial ground with plaques of people's names, benches, site-specific artifacts, etc. Instead we propose an annual "September 11 Event" of global gathering, a day when people come together, actually and virtually, at the site to mourn, exchange ideas, communicate, exhibit, perform, and simply be with one another.

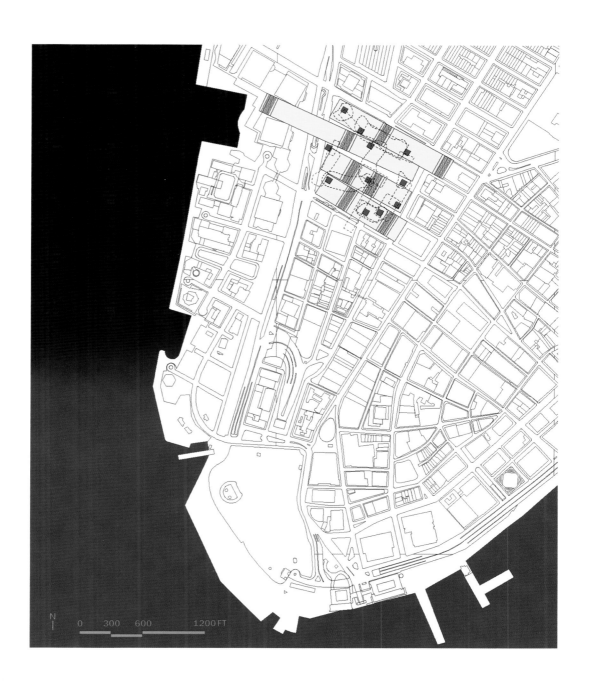

N
0   300   600   1200 FT

Every year on September 11 these towers would weep by transmitting a mist from their skins (using a sprinkler system). As an event this memorial would not only help people to heal, it would offer a much deeper ceremony, intensely personal and emotionally powerful.

As years go by, and even if people stop showing up, New York as a city can easily absorb a surreal day, once a year, when 11 towers weep and no passerby knows why

COMMERCIAL

PRIVATE EQUITY OFFICES

2007

LOCATION: **MIDTOWN, NEW YORK CITY, NEW YORK, USA**
TOTAL AREA: **14,000 SQUARE FEET**
PROGRAM: **EXECUTIVE OFFICES, TRADERS' BULLPEN AREA, LARGE CONFERENCE ROOMS, SERVICE RECEPTION, AND WAITING AREAS**
STATUS: **COMPLETED 2007**

This fast-growing investment and advisory firm was expanding from a partial floor to a full floor of a midtown Manhattan office building. They were looking for a timeless, elegant, and efficient office that would allow them to move to their new space within a six-month design and construction time line.

The new 14,500-gross-square-foot space accommodates four different groups: capital partners, capital advisors, capital management, and real estate. The challenge was to recognize and accommodate each group's independent needs yet encourage interrelation and exchange of information between groups while maintaining a coherent whole.

An L-shaped plan with an open center and clear, efficient circulation defines the organization of the floor plan. Timeless, environmentally sustainable materials and the use of natural light throughout the space brings a sense of continuity and transparency to this office. The entire floor is raised for flexibility and individual control of air circulation. It is also environmentally friendly, allowing the whole floor to become a giant duct, in turn allowing higher ceilings in most parts of the space. As this raised floor covers the existing heating units and the spandrel glass, the line where the floor and curtain wall meet is blurred, affording a feeling of floating above the city.

The lobby/reception and waiting areas are defined by dark-wood folding planes, giving identity and providing lighting and tactility to each space. Executive offices are behind a wall of translucent glass. This wall not only brings natural light into the main hallway, it also brings color and texture to the space. A large boardroom seating 20 people marks one corner of the space and is directly accessible from the waiting area while the CEO's office marks the other corner. A linear transparent pod holds the kitchen, copy center, research room, and the administration. These spaces can be closed for privacy or remain open via a series of sliding panels and doors. The bullpen/open space area, approximately one third of the floor, is flooded with natural light and has collaborative stations with access to a variety of smaller meeting/conference rooms.

1 ELEVATOR LOBBY
2 RECEPTION
3 WAITING AREA
4 ADMINISTRATIVE STAFF
5 OFFICE
6 CEO'S OFFICE
7 PANTRY
8 COPY/SUPPLY
9 LIBRARY
10 BOARDROOM
11 CONFERENCE ROOM
12 OPEN AREA
13 BATHROOM
14 SERVER ROOM

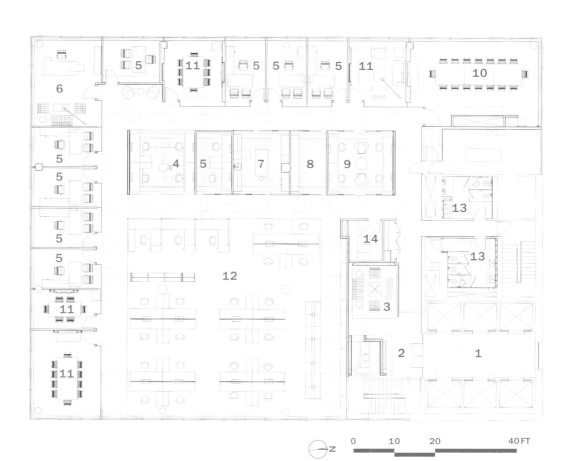

0   10   20   40 FT

The lobby/reception and waiting areas are defined by "folding planes." These folding planes in dark wood create a sculptural identity, providing lighting and facility to each space.

Executive offices are behind a wall of translucent glass

This project creates a thoughtful, forward-looking environment that combines the refinements of a home with the efficiency of an office space, a place for creative thinking and working long hours

A large boardroom seating 20 people marks one corner of the space

UNIFIED FIELD OFFICES

2001

LOCATION: **NEW YORK CITY, NEW YORK, USA**
TOTAL AREA: **5,000 SQUARE FEET**
PROGRAM: **WORKSTATION AREA, SMALL LIBRARY, LOUNGE,**
CONFERENCE/MULTIMEDIA ROOM, RECEPTION, KITCHEN
STATUS: **COMPLETED 2001**

This 5,000-square-foot space in New York City's Silicon Alley area is kept mainly as a large, open loft/studio space to accommodate the needs of Unified Field, a growing software and multimedia design company. Its mission to translate data into information and information into insight became the inspiration for this project.

The main architectural element of the Unified Field offices is a composition of three curvilinear workstations defining three distinct but interrelated areas for the designers, programmers, and the development group. These workstations are constructed with aluminum, Lexan, and Plexiglas and act as a filter for light and a veil providing privacy, revealing only shadows of what is behind. This play of light and shadow, concave and convex, inside and outside, and actual and virtual information is on display throughout the whole space, creating a dynamic and inspiring work environment.

A rectilinear reception desk, with sliding panels displaying Unified Field's work, greets visitors upon entry. A translucent wall at one end begins the composition of the workstations and the translucent sliding panels on the other end reveal a conference/multimedia room and a lounge behind.

All mechanical ducts and the wiring cable tray are exposed in a centralized spine stretching from north to south, connecting the work area to the meeting rooms.

Unified Field's belief that communication isn't static in our quickly changing world and the need for flexible systems was the mission of this architecture.

1 ENTRY
2 RECEPTION
3 OFFICE
4 LOUNGE
5 CONFERENCE ROOM
6 FILES / WORK AREA
7 KITCHEN AREA
8 DESIGNERS
9 PROGRAMMERS
10 DEVELOPMENT

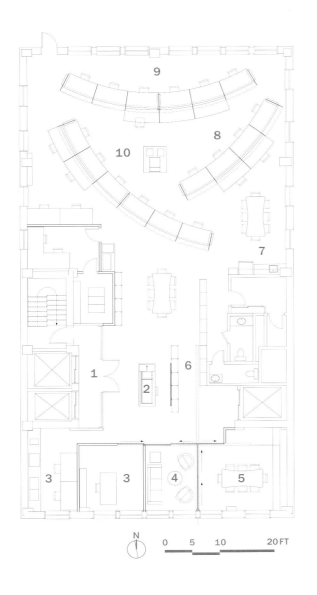

A translucent sculptural wall on one end begins the composition of the workstations

A rectilinear reception desk greets visitors upon entry

A translucent sliding panel displaying Unified Field's work reveals a conference/multimedia room and a lounge behind

EPICENTER MALL PROTOTYPE

2001

CLIENT: **GORDON/BRANT LLP**
LOCATION: **URBAN AREAS AND SUBURBAN MALLS**
TOTAL AREA: **150,000 SQUARE FEET**
PROGRAM: **45 TENANTS (APPROXIMATELY 3,000 SQUARE FEET EACH)**
STATUS: **SCHEMATIC DESIGN**

This project is a prototype of a 21st-century shopping mall that focuses on the utilization of new technology in retail. Here the deployment of high-tech devices and displays works in conjunction with a new distribution infrastructure to reorganize the space of shopping in the new millennium.

On the exterior, a glass curtain wall lit with LED lighting combined with a digital display system offers advertising, entertainment, information, color, and changing graphics, making this shopping mall's architecture dynamic and alive.

As shoppers enter the double-story-height retail atrium, a scanning device not only takes photographs and displays them on screens but it also sends the information regarding the shopper's size and preferred colors and designs to all the different stores and vendors.

To make the Epi Centers feasible and efficient, especially in tight urban areas, all the storage facilities are kept separate in large warehouses. Most vendors and stores will have only one of each item they are selling at the store, but virtually they have their whole collection on display screens. This way the shopper will actually see the color, touch the texture, feel the fabric and if their required size is not available then virtually try them on via digital displays. This will allow the buyer to become a model exhibited on large screens throughout the Epi Center.

Finally the most interesting concept of the shopping mall is the delivery of the purchased items to the desired location, home, office, or elsewhere. With a scanning device, shoppers purchase an item and the distribution infrastructure will deliver it to the specified location within six to eight hours. It is a hybrid of mall shopping and catalogue or online shopping. Imagine shopping without carrying the bags!

Architecturally the traditional department store layout of separate floors for separate goods has been reorganized and each floor will have a mix of merchandise from clothing to accessories, flatware, furniture, music, art, and more next to one another and on the same floor. The circulation is clearly marked by a lit glass floor that is always visible, evoking fashion runways and displaying the shoppers as models.

Its unique design, glamorous interiors, comfortable shopping, and entertaining experience is what makes this mall of the 21st century a destination for all visitors.

SITE:

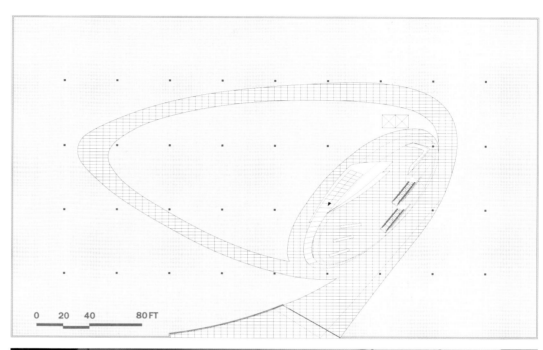

0 20 40   80 FT

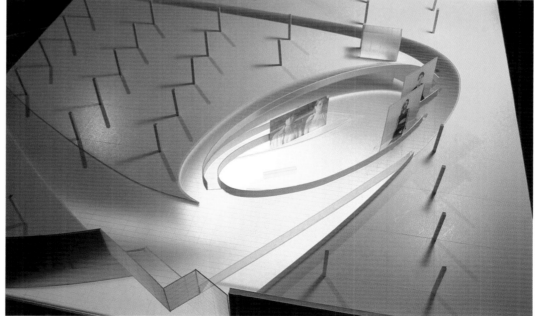

As shoppers enter the double-story-height
retail atrium, a scanning device not only takes
photographs and displays them on screens but it
also sends the information regarding the shopper's
size and preferred colors and designs to all the
different stores and vendors

The circulation is clearly marked by a lit glass floor that is always visible,
evoking fashion runways, displaying the shoppers as models

ISSEY MIYAKE TRIBECA

2000

LOCATION: **TRIBECA, NEW YORK CITY, NEW YORK, USA**
TOTAL AREA: **10,000 SQUARE FEET**
PROGRAM: **SHOWROOM, OFFICE, STORAGE**
STATUS: **INVITED COMPETITION**

Our vision for the Issey Miyake Showroom in Tribeca was to create a fluid space, vertically folding and connecting two floors. Here, what is elemental is the use of light as matter, the most minimal medium that has a profound physicality in the perception and experience of space.

Our thoughts for this proposal are organized around a number of concepts: transparency, continuity, and archaeology. The intention with these concepts is to investigate the relationship between the two disciplines via body and space and to blur the boundary between the two. Through this blurring, the experience and interaction of different but interrelated elements, from fabric to space, becomes evident.

A curved vertical plane connecting two floors creates a fluid space

TUIPRANICH SHOWROOM

2000

LOCATION: **MIAMI DESIGN DISTRICT, FLORIDA, USA**
TOTAL AREA: **5,000 SQUARE FEET**
PROGRAM: **FURNITURE SHOWROOM, DISPLAY AREA, RECEPTION AREA, SMALL OFFICES, STORAGE**
STATUS: **COMPLETED 2000**

This 5,000-square-foot space is kept open and loft-like, simple, austere, and sensual. Shallow pools of water surround the space, creating a metaphorical island. The water element also connects the space to its location (Miami Beach), and creates an environment that transforms and transcends the very idea of a showroom.

The aim is to create a total environment, celebrating inventive design, display, and furniture. Keeping the floor rather empty and quiet, the whole floor then becomes a stage for exhibition and spectatorship. The restraint in displaying furniture not only creates an austere setting, it also suggests the content of the store as precious objects.

On the exterior, the windows have been pushed out of the existing building line, wrapping around the space and completing the street corner. This extended horizontal curtain wall offers continuity to the street and is juxtaposed by a vertical double-story entrance portal.

The main element of the interior is a 50-foot-long wall of concrete and wood containing the reception desk, display area, and a narrow pool of water. This wall embraces visitors entering the space, and serves as the main backdrop for the displayed objects.

1 ENTRY
2 RECEPTION DESK
3 DISPLAY AREA
4 WORK ROOM/STORAGE
5 OFFICE

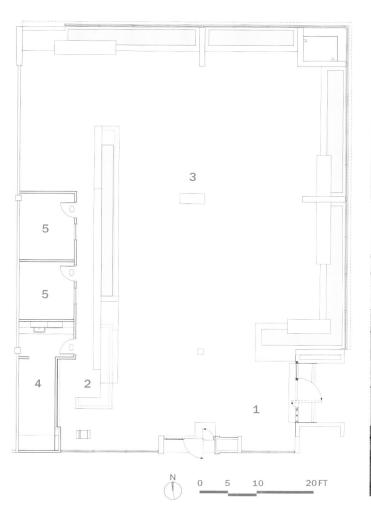

The main element of the interior is a 50-foot-long wall of concrete and wood, containing the reception desk, display area, and a narrow pool of water.

Shallow pools of water surrounding the space create a metaphorical island

JSM

1992

MUSIC STUDIOS

LOCATION: **NEW YORK CITY, NEW YORK, USA**
TOTAL AREA: **10,000 SQUARE FEET**
PROGRAM: **ADMINISTRATIVE OFFICES, RECORDING STUDIOS, RECEPTION AND WAITING AREA, LARGE CENTRAL LOUNGE FOR MEETINGS AND CONCERTS, KITCHEN AND DINING FACILITIES, BATHROOMS**
STATUS: **COMPLETED 1992**

The JSM Music Studios occupies 10,000 square feet and two floors of an industrial building in Manhattan. The scope of work was 4,500 square feet to accommodate the following program: new entry and logo, reception and waiting area, administrative offices, a large central lounge for meeting and concerts, kitchen and dining facilities, bathrooms, furniture and lighting, and a staircase connecting the two floors.

A series of repetitive cubical elements creates a rhythm in the space, which is 12 feet high by 5 feet wide and 112 feet long. Juxtaposed with this order on the opposite side of the space is a curvilinear system of "melodic" planes. The "rhythm" and "melody," the cubical elements and the curvilinear planes, come together in a dynamic space activated by a staircase to an upper level. This articulation molds the space into an instrument-like chamber where movement through the walls is similar to the movement of sound through a musical instrument.

Marking the entrance is the JSM Logo in the form of a hologram. Taking cues from the light-recording nature of holograms, the idea here is to record sound, light, and space.

The mechanical duct system and electrical cable tray are exposed, defining the main spine of the project. A display area for musical instruments and a bar area are carved into the curvilinear wall system providing auxiliary "hangout" spaces. The lounge and concert area is defined by a sheet of steel. Serving this space are three types of custom-designed furniture pieces: Galileo stools, an Amoeboid table, and Cloud Lights in strategic spaces throughout the melody of this project.

1 ENTRY/ELEVATOR LOBBY
2 HOLOGRAM LOGO
3 RECEPTION
4 OFFICES
5 ARTISTS' RECORDING ROOMS
6 MUSICAL DISPLAY AREA
7 BATHROOM
8 LOUNGE
9 KITCHEN
10 STAIRS TO UPPER FLOOR

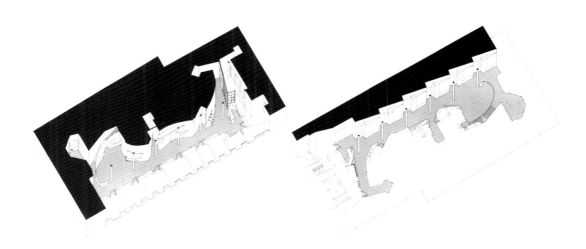

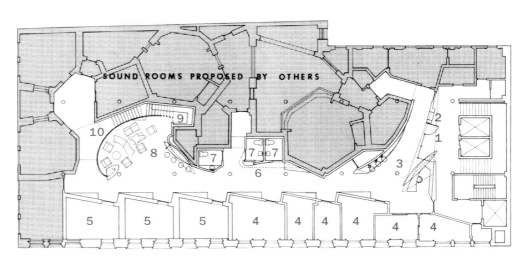

The lounge is a dynamic space activated by a staircase to an upper level

Marking the entrance is a stone reception desk penetrating through the entry wall

A curvilinear system of melodic planes begins at the entry

CULTURAL

MUSEUM OF 21ST CENTURY

2003

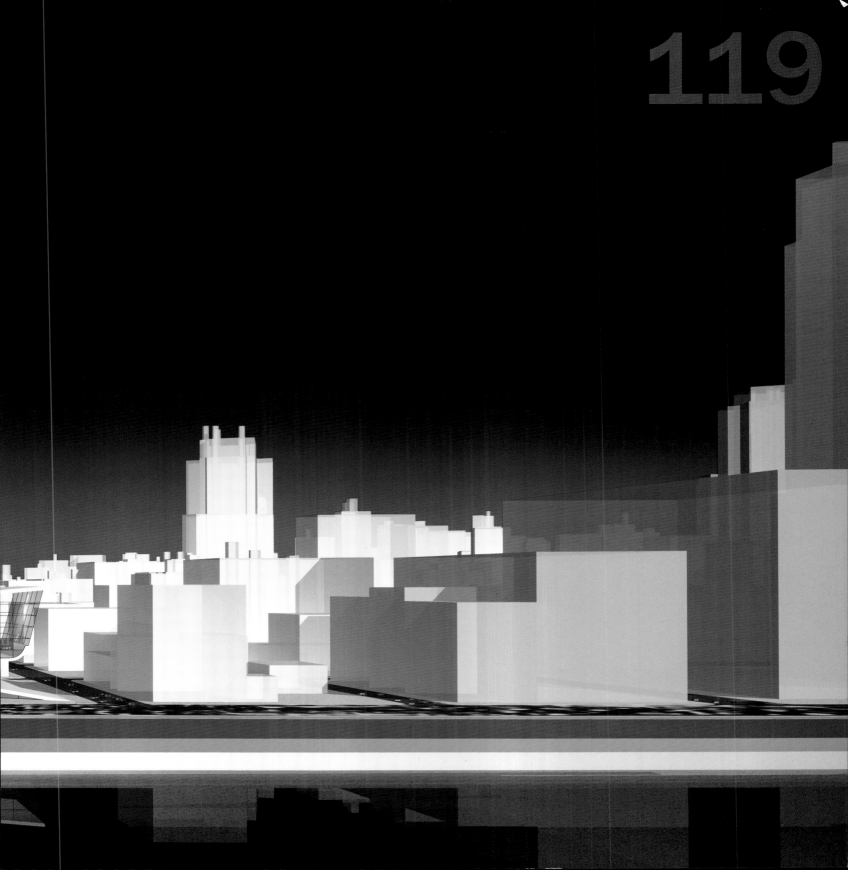

LOCATION: **NEW YORK CITY, NEW YORK, USA**
SITE: **TWO MANHATTAN BLOCKS**
TOTAL AREA: **750,000 SQUARE FEET**
PROGRAM: **TOWER A—41 FLOORS OF RESIDENTIAL CONDO; TOWER B—55 FLOORS OF OFFICES, 4 FLOORS OF MUSEUM SPACE (232,188 SQUARE FEET); AUDITORIUM ON 5TH FLOOR (15,845 SQUARE FEET)**
STATUS: **DESIGN PHASE**

In the new millennium, museums are no longer just "cabinets of curiosity" creating surprise and delight in palace-like settings, nor are they considered as a sacred space or a temple for art. Today, museums have become more like entertainment centers providing a variety of activities, from shopping to eating to performances, in a similar way to theme parks.

As contemporary culture and art changes and we become an increasingly global community equipped with digital technology and telecommunication networks, museums are becoming more like interdisciplinary forums with vast arrays of activities: social, political, cultural, technological, and educational. With art and mediums of making art drastically changed, we envision the architecture of 21st-century museums would no longer be a neutral box. A new museum should be an innovative space responding to new mediums and definitions of art.

This museum is vertical, not horizontal. It is a museum as an "interface" available to all artists. Here the museum concept has been turned inside-out, the boundaries between the content and its container are blurred and the thresholds between private and public, art and architecture, are re-examined.

Finally, the Museum of 21st Century is a place where the public can be challenged, conventions examined, and ideas presented. Its architecture reflects the notion of flexibility, possibilities, and inclusiveness through its spatial complexity and technological integration. It is an environment that stimulates art and enhances our experience and vision.

SITE:

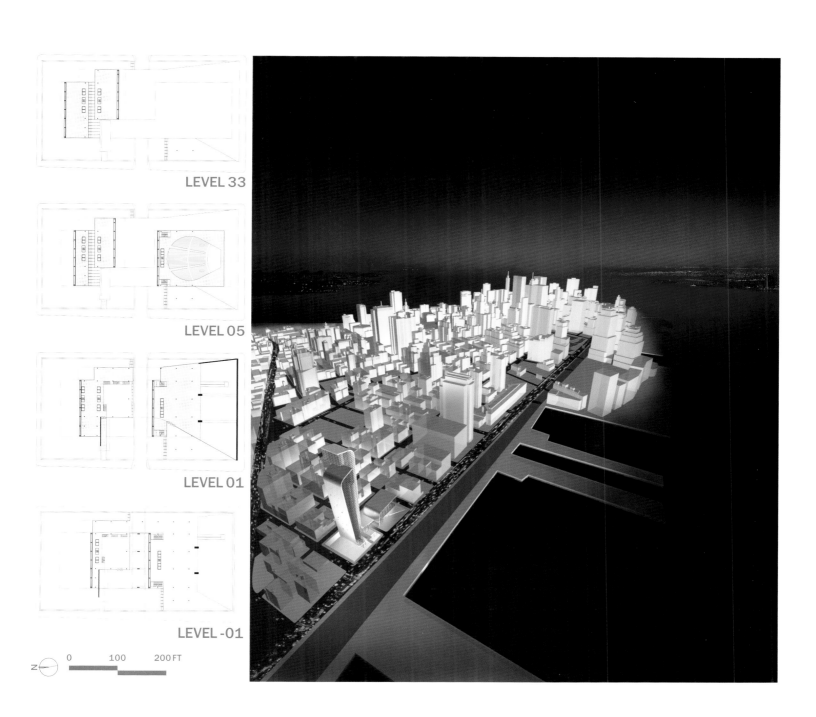

LEVEL 33

LEVEL 05

LEVEL 01

LEVEL -01

N

0   100   200 FT

This is a museum that is vertical,
not horizontal

Equipped with digital technology and telecommunication networks, museums are becoming more like interdisciplinary forums with vast arrays of activities

A new museum would be an innovative space responding to the new mediums and definition of art

It is a museum as an "interface" available to all artists

ROCA NEW YORK 2000

ROCKLAND CENTER FOR THE ARTS

LOCATION: **WEST NYACK, NEW YORK, USA**
SITE: **10 ACRES**
TOTAL AREA: **26,000 SQUARE FEET**
PROGRAM: **REGIONAL GALLERY, DIGITAL ART GALLERY, EXHIBITION SPACE FOR TRAVELING ART, MULTI-PURPOSE LECTURE/PERFORMANCE SPACE, NEW ADDITIONAL STUDIOS, SCULPTURE GARDEN, RENOVATION AND INCORPORATION OF THE EXISTING SCHOOL**
STATUS: **DESIGN DEVELOPMENT PHASE**

Situated in West Nyack, New York, the Rockland Center for the Arts offers its immediate community diverse programs, including exhibitions, concerts, art classes, children's activities, lectures, and symposia. It was founded in 1948 by luminaries Helen Hays, Maxwell Anderson, Kurt Weil, and Lotte Lenya.

As the arts center was expanding its vision and mission to become a major cultural center in the region, Hariri & Hariri were chosen from a shortlist of 37 reputable architectural firms to prepare a master plan including a new fine arts museum building with a variety of exhibition spaces, new additional studios, renovation and incorporation of the existing school, and a sculpture garden.

The proposed master plan will transform the 10-acre site into a park-like setting with a new museum building, not just creating a new entrance but what is essentially a profound and embracing experience of arrival. This new perception of the center is created via two new curved buildings as a fresh face to the whole complex. Like two arms, they embrace visitors and guide them inside, making the center a welcoming destination for the community and tourists to the Hudson Valley area.

This cultural destination, marked by two curved sculptural volumes and a meditative sculpture garden upon arrival, exhibits a digital sign embedded into one of the volumes. This LED display system will carry the center's logo and will forecast its daily activities, local news, and artistic announcements. The two volumes are connected by a transparent void that acts as the new lobby and reception area, and provides access to all the galleries and the school behind them. The 26,000-square-foot expansion will offer the first fine arts museum in Rockland County. It will consist of a regional gallery, digital art gallery, and a 5,000-square-foot exhibition space for traveling art exhibitions.

1 EXISTING BUILDING
2 NEW BUILDING PHASE I
3 NEW BUILDING PHASE II
4 SCULPTURE GARDEN
5 COURTYARD/AMPHITHEATER
6 PARKING
7 TENT
8 PLAY AREA
9 POOL
10 CARETAKER'S HOUSE

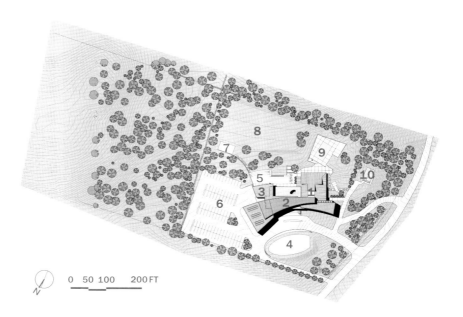

0 50 100   200 FT

In addition, the new building will provide a multi-purpose lecture and performance space that converts into meeting and executive conference areas. It will open onto an outdoor amphitheater for performances and summer concerts. The museum galleries and performance areas are supported by a museum shop, an indoor/outdoor café, and a variety of spaces for exhibition, installations, projection, and digital art. The existing school and art studios will be renovated and an additional computer laboratory, as well as ceramic, sculpture, and jewelry-making studios will be provided.

A landscaped parking facility for 100 cars is planned at the end of the driveway behind the new building. This will provide direct access to the large sculpture park in the back and walkways through the property will link with the adjacent state park.

Finally the architecture of the new center expresses this dynamic organization and will provide a place where artists can develop their skills, exhibit, perform, teach, study, work, innovate, and present their work to the public in an inspiring and dynamic environment.

An outdoor amphitheater for performances and summer concerts is supported by an indoor/outdoor café, and variety of spaces for exhibition, installations, projection, and digital art

The museum will consist of exhibition space for regional, digital, and traveling art

The two volumes are connected with a transparent void that acts as the new lobby and reception area, and provides access to the galleries and the school behind them

CINE

FILM CENTER

1999

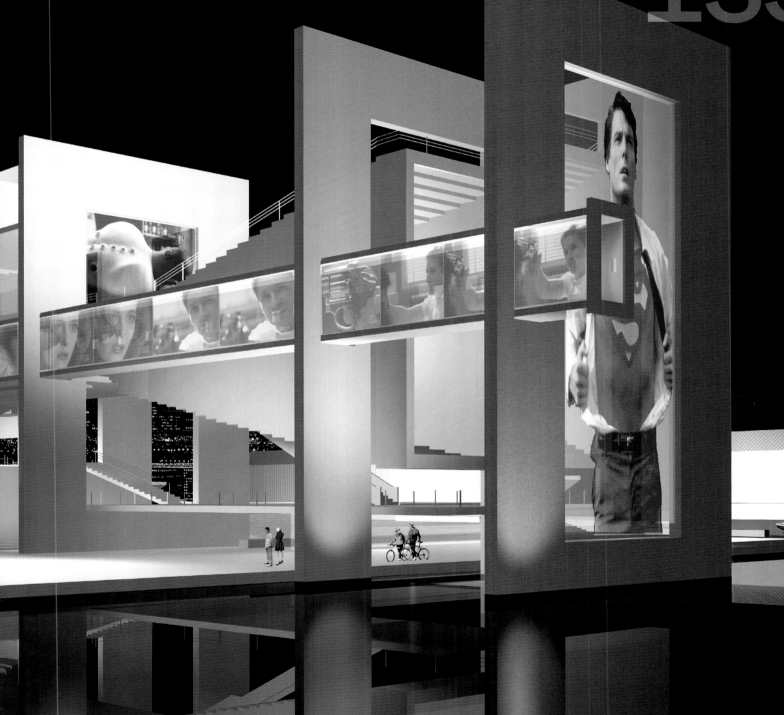

LOCATION: **BROOKLYN HEIGHTS, NEW YORK, USA**
SITE: **PIER #2 UNDER BROOKLYN BRIDGE**
TOTAL AREA: **54,000 SQUARE FEET**
PROGRAM: **FILM SCHOOL—12,647 SQUARE FEET; INDOOR CINEMAS—7,760 SQUARE FEET;**
OUTDOOR CINEMAS—6,728 SQUARE FEET; EXHIBITION—2,323 SQUARE FEET;
DECK #1—11,351 SQUARE FEET; DECK #2—4,250 SQUARE FEET;
CAFÉ—6,022 SQUARE FEET; PROMENADE—33,962 SQUARE FEET;
FILM FESTIVAL THEATER—4,000 SQUARE FEET
STATUS: **DESIGN PHASE**

The Experimental Film Center, located on a pier near the base of the Brooklyn Bridge in New York, is to be completed in the year 2020. This complex explores the relationship of architecture and film through its form and structure, and the nature of entertainment in the new millennium.

With digital technology already changing the process of photography and an abundance of new digital video technology being introduced to the entertainment and communication markets, one can only imagine how the film and the movie industry will change in the near future.

In the Experimental Film Center the screens can be seen from the street and the river and are made of Digital Micromirror Device (DMD) technology. These screens can be programmed to display information, receive and show films via satellite, and act as projection screens. Virtual actors, virtual sets, and locations are all stored within and can be reconfigured into a new movie at any time.

This complex is a pier structure with a series of structural concrete frames supporting different parts of the program. A digital screen on the Brooklyn side displays previews of films and marks the entrance to the film school and the complex. The school structure is a rectangular box containing classrooms, screening and editing rooms, and sound studios, offering state-of-the-art technology and equipment for filmmaking.

The Film Track Gallery is a long tube accessed by a spiral ramp from the street and is open to the public. This gallery exhibits filmstrips on its DMD, which can be viewed from both the inside and the benches on the plaza outside.

In the center of the structure three theaters with vertical and horizontal digital screens challenge common screen dimensions and offer possibilities for changing the format of new movies. At the end of the pier is a large indoor/outdoor theater for film festivals with the DMD screen detached from the structure. This screen facing Manhattan also caters to the sailors and people arriving at the pier by boat and is reminiscent of the drive-in cinemas that were popular half a century ago.

1 DECK #1
2 DECK #2
3 CYBER CAFÉ
4 OUTDOOR CAFÉ
5 PROMENADE
6 PARKING
7 FILM SCHOOL
8 OUTDOOR CINEMA
9 EXHIBITION
10 INDOOR CINEMA

Interwoven with the architecture of this new-millennium film-and-entertainment center are covered shooting galleries with ramps and bridges for use as film locations and variety of public spaces for meditation and observation. Finally, a large video arcade and cyber café enclosed in glass brings together the next generation of filmmakers.

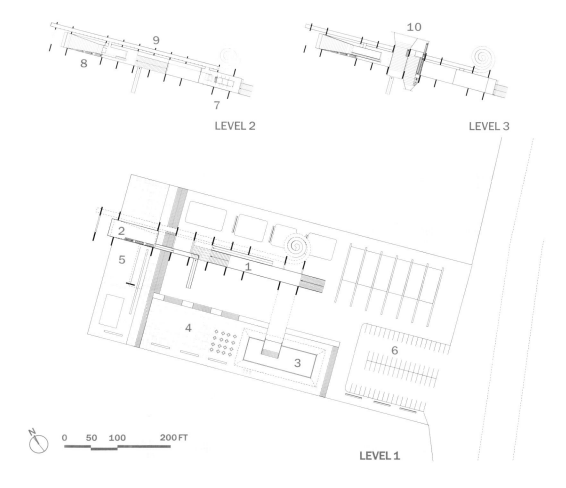

LEVEL 2

LEVEL 3

0   50   100   200 FT

LEVEL 1

A digital screen on the Brooklyn side displays previews of films and marks the entrance to the film school and the complex

The Film Track Gallery is a long tube accessed by a spiral ramp from the street and is open to the public

The screen facing Manhattan also caters to the sailors and people arriving to the pier by boat, reminiscent of the drive-in cinemas that were popular half a century ago

This complex is a pier structure with a series of structural concrete frames holding different parts of its program.

Interwoven with the architecture of this film-and-entertainment center are covered shooting galleries with ramps and bridges for use as film locations

KOMA

LOS ANGELES

1995

LOCATION: **LOS ANGELES (KOREATOWN), CALIFORNIA, USA**
SITE: **1.9 ACRES (257 BY 322 FEET)**
TOTAL AREA: **204,000 SQUARE FEET**
PROGRAM: **MUSEUM ART GALLERIES—32,000 SQUARE FEET; PERFORMANCE HALL—16,000 SQUARE FEET; LIBRARY—12,000 SQUARE FEET; LECTURE HALL—4,000 SQUARE FEET; STUDIOS—8,000 SQUARE FEET; GARDEN/COURTYARD—12,000 SQUARE FEET; PARKING—240 CARS**
STATUS: **COMPETITION ENTRY**

After the riots of 1993 in Los Angeles, the Korean–American population had to face the reality that they needed to establish a harmonious relationship with other ethnic communities, so the objective was to design an inviting center that would share the richness of Korean culture with others in the neighborhood.

Inspired by traditional Korean structures, gates, gardens, and bells, we designed an inviting cultural center as a place for pause or a rest from the world around, regardless of ethnicity, a place of awakening, a place of dawn.

The program includes a museum building, a garden/courtyard, a large library and a performance hall.

In this proposal, the experience of KOMA begins with the garden, the focus and heart of the project. Centralized and always present to the visitor's view, the garden acts as the organizer of the whole project. The different parts of the program are treated as clear and distinct volumes articulated around the garden and connected by continuous circuits of circulation slabs.

The soul of KOMA is the performance hall; this large parabolic volume rises from a rectilinear base and counterbalances the void of the garden. This dichotomy between solid and void becomes the driving force of the project. The corner of the complex is distinctly marked by a monumental curved wall, which is the cornerstone of the project, where the founders' names will be placed. Finally, the contemporary sculpture gallery is a bridge-like structure acting as a light beacon above the garden, celebrating the new Korean–American generation in America.

1 COURTYARD
2 ENTRY LOBBY / RECEPTION
3 GIFT SHOP
4 LECTURE HALL
5 RESTAURANT
6 BAR
7 PERFORMANCE HALL
8 LIBRARY
9 EXHIBITION ROOM
10 OPEN TO BELOW

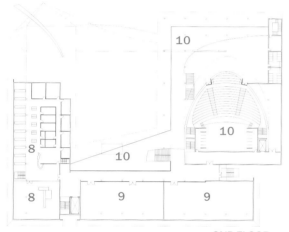

2ND FLOOR

1ST FLOOR

0   30   60   120 FT

The corner of this complex is distinctly marked by a monumental curved wall—the cornerstone of the project

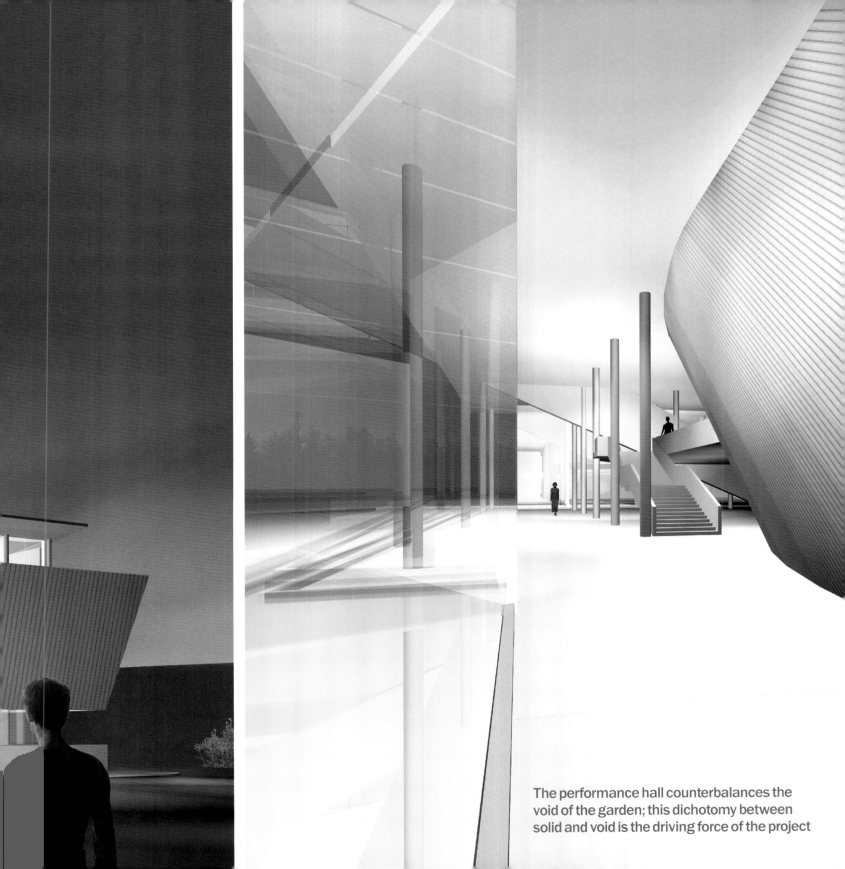

The performance hall counterbalances the void of the garden; this dichotomy between solid and void is the driving force of the project

The courtyard / garden is centralized and always in view and acts as the organizer of the whole project

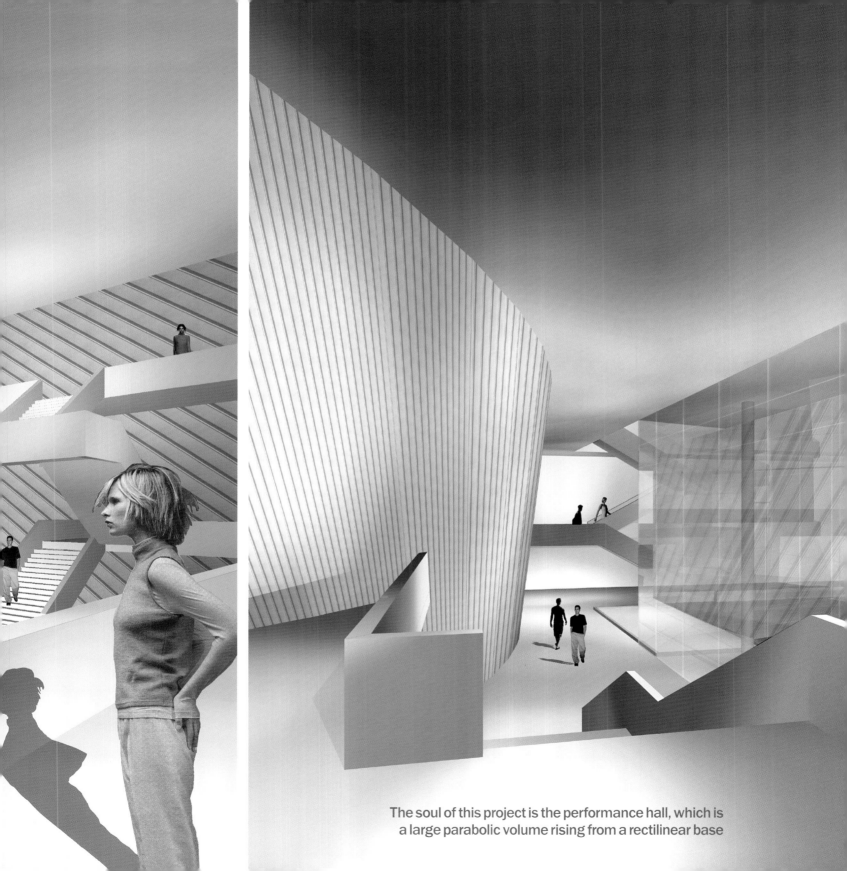

The soul of this project is the performance hall, which is
a large parabolic volume rising from a rectilinear base

HOSPITALITY

HIGHLINE HOTEL

2007

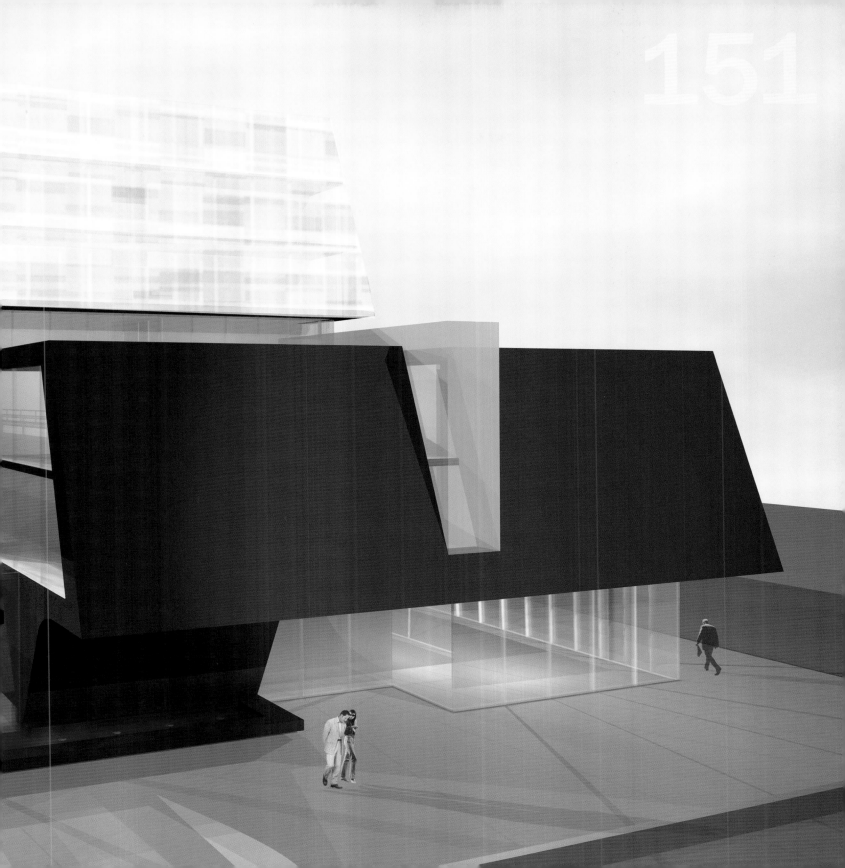

LOCATION: CHELSEA DISTRICT, NEW YORK CITY, NEW YORK, USA
SITE: 169–183 TENTH AVENUE
TOTAL AREA: 92,000 SQUARE FEET
PROGRAM: BOUTIQUE HOTEL WITH 140 ROOMS, GALLERY SPACE AND RETAIL AREAS
STATUS: DESIGN PHASE

The High Line Hotel is an exclusive boutique hotel planned in the Chelsea area, the heart of New York City's art galleries. It is located on a site adjacent to the celebrated elevated park on the abandoned railway known as the High Line. It stretches 184 feet along 10th Avenue and is surrounded by prime art galleries.

The main entrance to the hotel is through a side street, intentionally hidden and discreet to ensure visitors' privacy and providing the experience of discovering a surreal oasis in the big concrete city.

The hotel's design was inspired by its architectural context, the local bohemian culture, and the industrial steel structure of the elevated railway running along the back of the site. Three distinct volumes contain different parts of the hotel, which are articulated with different materials in response to its surrounding structures.

The volume on 10th Avenue contains the gallery/retail space and a restaurant and is enclosed by mainly transparent glass, making it visible to pedestrians on the street. The two floors above street level have a repetitive window system in dark steel exhibiting the guest rooms on the avenue. At this level the hotel connects with the High Line park at the back and its dark steel façade creates a dynamic relationship between the old and new structures.

The top three levels of this hotel float on top of a recessed section and are wrapped in a curtain wall offering panoramic views of the neighborhood. A large roof terrace and a variety of hotel amenities are located on top of the third floor offering indoor/outdoor activities and a place to become part of the voyeuristic city.

The two floors above street level have a repetitive window system in dark steel exhibiting the guest rooms on the avenue

The main entrance to the hotel is through a side street, intentionally hidden and discreet

HOTEL DUBAI

2007

LOCATION: **BUSINESS BAY, DUBAI, UNITED ARAB EMIRATES**
SITE: **23,646 SQUARE FEET**
TOTAL AREA: **502,063 SQUARE FEET**
PROGRAM: **33-STORY TOWERS CONTAINING 220 HOTEL ROOMS AND 129 FULL-SERVICE LUXURY RESIDENCES; SKY LOBBY; SIGNATURE RESTAURANT; SPA; FITNESS CENTER; SWIMMING FACILITIES; MEETING ROOMS; BALLROOMS, BAR/LOUNGE SPACE; ROOFTOP GARDEN; 5-STORY PODIUM CONTAINING EXCLUSIVE BOUTIQUES, RESTAURANTS, BALLROOMS, BUSINESS CENTER, AND TWO FLOORS OF PARKING UNDERGROUND**
STATUS: **DESIGN PHASE**

Located in a newly developed mixed-use district conceived by Dubai Properties called Dubai Business Bay Center, this signature tower is composed of two laser-cut metal screens draped like a veil on the east and west façades. These lattice-like skins have a geometric arabesque pattern and were inspired by the area's traditional musharabias, providing views and privacy at the same time. They create dramatic patterns of light and shadow inside and outside this tower, especially at night. On the north and south the tower is wrapped in a transparent glass façade, maximizing the panoramic views.

A sky-lobby on the 22nd floor receives hotel guests and the top 10 floors are to be occupied by a luxury hotel brand. A signature restaurant and a spa/wellness center are located on the top floors of the tower servicing both the hotel guests and the residences. The 20 floors below the hotel lobby are luxury, fully serviced, 1-, 2-, and 3-bedroom apartments with access to a roof garden and a swimming pool. The podium section acts as the base of the tower and contains the ballrooms, business center, and exclusive boutiques. Two full floors below ground accommodate parking and a variety of services catering to both hotel and residences.

1 SERVICES
2 HOTEL AMENITIES
3 HOTEL ROOMS
4 SERVICED RESIDENCES
5 BALLROOM/BANQUET HALLS
6 PARKING
7 RESTAURANT/BAR
8 REFLECTING POOL
9 APARTMENT LOBBY
10 DROP-OFF AREA
11 HOTEL LOBBY
12 HOTEL SKY-LOBBY

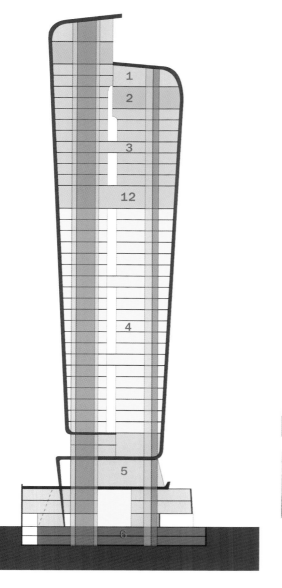

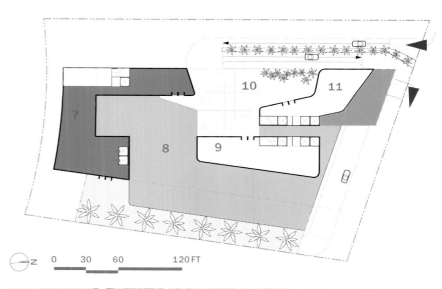

0 30 60 120 FT

JUAN VALDEZ FLAGSHIP

2004

LOCATION: **140 EAST 57TH STREET, NEW YORK CITY, NEW YORK, USA**
TOTAL AREA: **2,100 SQUARE FEET**
PROGRAM: **NEW BUILDING FAÇADE, SIGNAGE AND LOGO, NEW STOREFRONT, SERVING BAR, LOUNGE, BATHROOMS, OFFICE/STORAGE**
STATUS: **COMPLETED 2004**

For the Juan Valdez flagship in New York City the challenge was to create an architectural environment that would link the coffee growers in Colombia to consumers in the US. Fundamentally, this project had to address the overlap of two cultures (Colombia and USA), the spirit of Juan Valdez versus Generation X consumers, and nature versus technology.

We examined the three states of coffee: beans, granules, and liquid. Coffee in liquid form has an ephemeral aroma that creates a long-lasting memory directly connected to our sense of smell and sense of place.

A palette of complementary architectural materials reflects the different states evoked by coffee, such as exclusivity, warmth, timelessness, and boundlessness.

Architecturally, the street façade becomes the link between Colombia and New York with a stainless-steel screen stretched along the entire building with an abstract watermark image of Juan Valdez etched onto it. This brings a coherent identity to Juan Valdez and the building as a whole.

Conceptually, the storefront is a section cut through a coffee bean made of coffee-colored teak wood. The teak wood continues on the inside and becomes the spatial organizer, uniting the bar, the merchandising, and the lounge area.

As one walks in, there is a soft, free flowing "liquid wall" that continues through the entire length of the space and wraps around the lounge area at the end, with seating carved out into the wall. The liquid wall represents the liquidity and aroma of coffee, leaving a long-lasting impression on visitors.

1 CAFÉ ENTRANCE
2 TEAK WOOD PLATFORM
3 SERVING BAR
4 LOUNGE AREA
5 WC
6 STORAGE
7 SEPARATE ENTRY/LOBBY FOR UPPER FLOORS

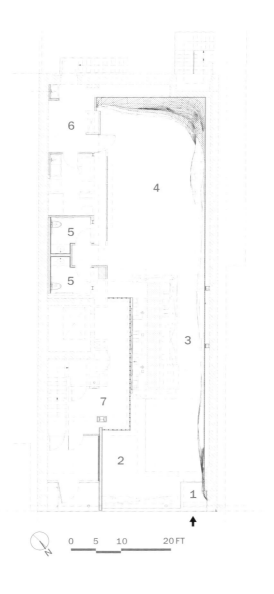

0 5 10 20 FT

The storefront is a section cut through a coffee bean made of coffee-colored teak wood

As one walks in, there is a soft, free-flowing liquid wall that continues through the entire length of the space, representing the liquidity and aroma of coffee and leaving a long-lasting impression on visitors

The liquid wall wraps around the lounge area at the end, with seating carved into the wall

TUTTLE STREET RESTAURANT

2002

LOCATION: **MIAMI DESIGN DISTRICT, FLORIDA, USA**
TOTAL AREA: **10,000 SQUARE FEET**
PROGRAM: **RESTAURANT, BAR AREA, ROOF TERRACE**
STATUS: **SCHEMATIC DESIGN**

Located in the Miami design district developed by visionary developer Craig Robins, this corner lot was allocated for a signature restaurant/bar space and to act as a gateway to the design center. This restaurant not only marks the entry but is also a place where artists, designers, gallery owners, buyers, and visitors can get together in the design district.

This 10,000-square-foot restaurant continues Miami's tradition of modern architecture, particularly its buildings from the historic art deco period. The corner entrance is marked and articulated with a curved volume containing a ramp to the upper level and the roof terrace above. This curved volume not only contains interior circulation, it also becomes an art object by exhibiting digital art on the exterior. A plaza with outdoor seating defines the entry area and is enclosed by the curved art wall.

A two-story glass façade at the entrance invites and welcomes visitors, while on the main boulevard a transparent base with sliding doors accomodates an indoor/outdoor café. The upper level offers a more solid volume providing a more private and quiet space for diners. An "oceanic volume" containing the bar cantilevers from the upper level, becoming the signage and a billboard to the street.

Finally, the aim is to provide variety of spaces for different activities and blur the threshold between private and public, inside and outside, past and future.

1 ENTRY
2 RESTAURANT
3 SIDEWALK CAFÉ
4 KITCHEN
5 RESTROOM
6 ART WALL
7 PLAZA
8 OCEANIC BAR

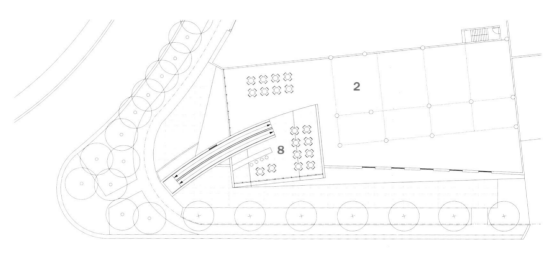

SECOND FLOOR PLAN

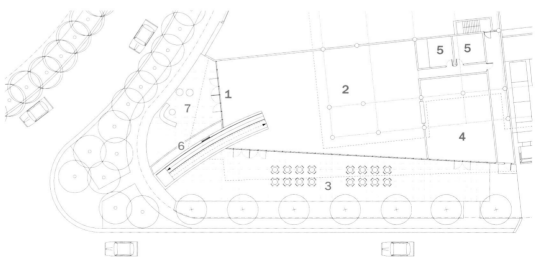

GROUND FLOOR PLAN

0   20   40   80 FT

The curved volume contains interior circulation
and becomes an art object exhibiting digital art
on the exterior

An "oceanic volume" containing the bar cantilevers from the
upper level, becoming the signage and a billboard to the street

RESIDENTIAL

SUTTON PLACE RESIDENCE

2005–2008

LOCATION: **MIDTOWN, NEW YORK CITY, NEW YORK, USA**
SITE: **TWO APARTMENTS ON THE 4TH FLOOR**
TOTAL AREA: **5,000 SQUARE FEET**
PROGRAM: **3 BEDROOMS, 6 BATHROOMS, LIVING ROOM, DINING ROOM, KITCHEN, FAMILY/MEDIA ROOM, GUESTROOM, 2 TERRACES**
STATUS: **COMPLETED 2008**

Located in the Sutton Place neighborhood of New York City, this 5,000-square-foot home is a combination of two adjacent apartments for a family of contemporary art collectors. As their children grew and needed more space, so did their exquisite art collection, which needed an exhibition space.

The existing structure of the building had created long and narrow spaces, making planning for the new apartment challenging. The two apartments connect at the family room via an opening in the concrete structural wall. The residence is then divided into two parts: the public side containing living, dining, kitchen, and powder room; and the private side with four bedroom/bathroom suites around a billiard room.

As one moves from the public side to the private quarters the floor material changes from stone to dark wood, what remains constant is the presence of art throughout the apartment.

Conceptually the whole dwelling is treated as a gallery space with walls to exhibit art. Gallery-like lighting and viewing space is interwoven within the architecture of this residence. A rectangular entry gallery exhibiting a sculptural wall in dark wood embraces visitors. An art wall exhibits a mural by Julian Opie and a translucent glass wall brings natural light into the entry area. This material composition continues throughout the apartment, creating a special continuity and visual connectivity.

The selected furniture is simple and sculptural, and at times becomes a work of art. For example, the coffee table is a floating glass cube supported by a series of organically shaped salvaged timber beams by John Houshmand, which was specifically commissioned for this residence. A long rectilinear chandelier from the Swarovski Crystal Palace collection complements a white lacquered cabinet cantilevered from the dining room wall. In the kitchen are zebrawood cabinets, with a wall of stainless steel containing the ovens and refrigerator. White statuary marble covers accent walls and eating counters. The family room acts as a media center and has a baby grand piano. Next to the family room is a private hall with a billiard table in the center and art on all walls. The entrance to all bedrooms is through this private hall.

1 ENTRY
2 KITCHEN
3 DINING ROOM
4 LIVING ROOM
5 FAMILY/MEDIA ROOM
6 BILLIARD ROOM
7 BEDROOM
8 MASTER BEDROOM
9 GUEST ROOM
10 TERRACE
11 MAID'S ROOM
12 BATHROOM
13 CLOSET

Finally, the master suite has a sleeping area, a sitting area, and a work station/desk area all in one space. The centerpiece of the room is a limestone bench and TV holder separating and connecting the different spaces at the same time. The master bathroom is in limestone with steps and a white pebble wall creating a Zen, spa-like space, for moments of peace, relaxation, and tranquility.

0   5   10   20 FT

The selected furniture is simple
and sculptural, and at times
becomes a work of art

A long rectilinear chandelier from the Swarovski Crystal Palace collection complements a white lacquered cabinet cantilevered from the wall in the dining room

182

White statuary marble covers
accent walls and eating counters

Cabinets are in zebrawood, with a wall of stainless steel containing the ovens and refrigerator

Next to the family room is a
private hall with a billiard table in
the center and art on all walls

The family room acts as a media center and has a baby grand piano

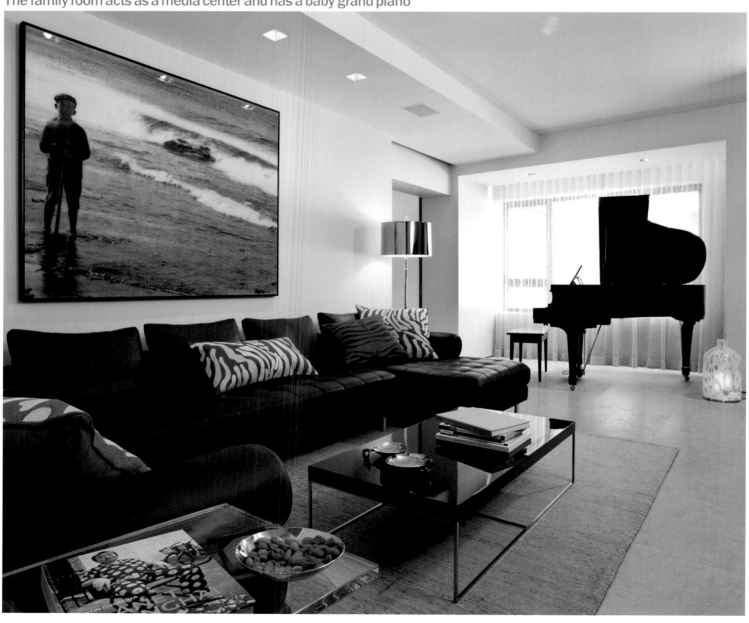

The master suite has a sleeping area, sitting area, and a work station/desk area all in one space. The centerpiece of the room is a limestone bench and TV holder separating and connecting the different spaces at the same time.

LIVE

YOUR MONEY AT RISK

2:00PM CT

WORLDWIDE INTEREST RATES CUT

HeadlineNews

Panasonic

CENTURY

L'ART NOUVEAU

The master bathroom is in limestone with steps and a white pebble wall creating a Zen, spa-like space, for moments of peace, relaxation, and tranquility

WILTON POOLHOUSE

2007

LOCATION: **WILTON, CONNECTICUT, USA**
TOTAL LOT AREA: **3.5 ACRES**
TOTAL POOLHOUSE AREA : **1,200 SQUARE FEET PLUS 3,630 SQUARE FEET OF POOL AND STONE TERRACE**
PROGRAM: **POOL, INDOOR/OUTDOOR SPACE, SPA, BATHROOM, KITCHEN/BAR**
STATUS: **COMPLETED 2007**

This 1,200-square-foot structure was designed as a minimalist sculpture in the landscape. It is part of a 3.5-acre property in Wilton, Connecticut. The architecture of this pool house is in contrast to the traditional architecture of the existing house, yet the design sets up a dialogue between the two.

The architecture of the pool house hovers over a 48- by 20-foot pool like a vessel in the water. To the north is a spa and an outdoor/indoor shower, and to the south a roofed veranda acts as an indoor/outdoor dining area with a large opening on the wall framing the landscape beyond. The area around the pool becomes a sunken courtyard paved in travertine with steps and walls of stone.

The main frame and the ceiling of the structure are ipe wood (Brazilian walnut) and make the place warm and nautical but connected to the landscape at the same time. The wood floors stretch out from the interior, floating over the pool and become a deck for reflecting and simply relaxing with your toes in the water. A fire pit on the south side of the structure creates an intimate space on the end of the terrace for cold-weather gatherings, toasting marshmallows, and enjoying the setting.

The interior of this pool house contains a living/entertainment room, a kitchen and bar area, a simple bathroom, and a variety of terraces and decks. It is enclosed by a series of metal-and-glass sliding panels that allow the structure to be transparent and open up to the outside. A wall of green mosaic tiles covers the wet areas (both inside and outside showers) and becomes part of the main composition of the façade, bringing color and tactility to the place.

EXISTING: OLD POOL AND STORAGE SHED
          MAIN HOUSE

1 POOL HOUSE
2 POOL DECK
3 POOL
4 SPA
5 FIRE PIT
6 MAIN HOUSE (EXISTING)
7 BARN (EXISTING)
8 DRIVEWAY

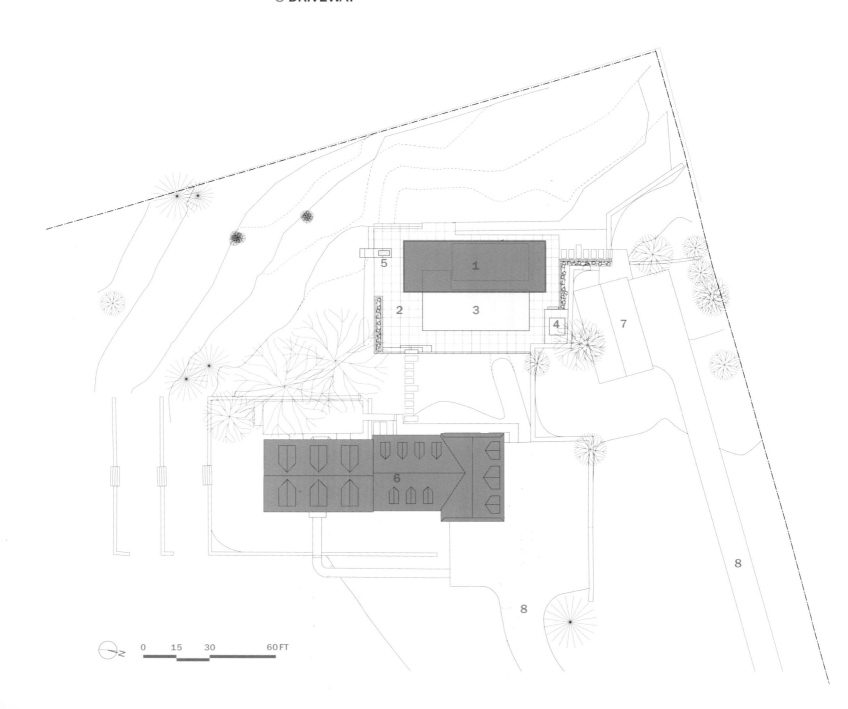

0 15 30 60 FT

1 POOL HOUSE
2 KITCHENETTE
3 BATH
4 UTILITY ROOM
5 OUTDOOR SHOWER
6 VERANDA
7 POOL DECK
8 POOL
9 SPA
10 FIRE PIT

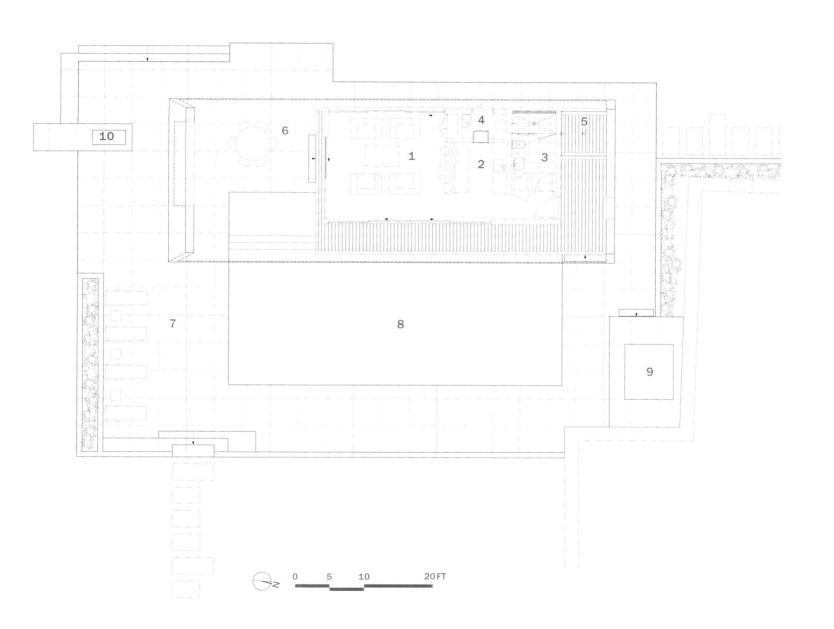

0   5   10   20 FT

The architecture of the pool house
hovers over the pool like a vessel
in the water

On the south a roofed veranda acts as
an indoor/outdoor dining area with a
large opening on the wall framing the
landscape beyond

The wood floors stretch out from the interior, floating over the pool and becoming a deck for reflecting and simply relaxing with your toes in the water

The main frame and the ceiling of the
structure are ipe wood and make the
place warm, nautical, and sculptural
at the same time

SAGAPONAC PAINTING STUDIO

2006

LOCATION: **EAST HAMPTON, LONG ISLAND, NEW YORK, USA**
SITE: **100-ACRE DEVELOPMENT**
TOTAL LOT AREA: **2.7 ACRES**
TOTAL STUDIO AREA: **900 SQUARE FEET, PLUS 1,100 SQUARE FEET PAVED TERRACE**
PROGRAM: **OPEN STUDIO SPACE, PRIVATE TERRACE, INDOOR BATHROOM, STORAGE, OUTDOOR SHOWER FOR POOL AREA, AND SEATING FOR TENNIS COURT**
STATUS: **COMPLETED 2006**

This 900-square-foot studio is located in Long Island, New York and is part of the Sagaponac House property. The main house was completed by Hariri & Hariri – Architecture in 2004 and the owners asked for an additional structure to be used as a painting studio that would complement the main house architecturally.

The painting studio continues the same design language but rather than adopting the volumetric composition of the main house, it begins with a planar composition of walls. Each wall of the studio responds to different parts of the site and is composed of a different material, creating an architectonic 'painting.'

The main façade facing the pool continues the material of the pool deck with a wall of travertine concealing an outdoor shower. Behind the travertine wall is a wall of blue mosaic tiles that continues through to the interior bathroom behind.

The main room is one large space with clerestories and skylights bringing in natural light yet allowing ample wall space to exhibit completed artwork. On the south side a wall of glass with large sliding panels opens to a private covered terrace, providing a place for contemplation.

On the west side, facing the tennis court, a long blank stucco wall stretches out like a blank canvas. This wall not only shields the structure from stray tennis balls, it also provides a bench for observing the game and a backdrop for the seating area.

Finally, this painting studio expresses a conceptual relationship between painting and architecture.

1 PAINTING STUDIO
2 SAGAPONAC HOUSE
3 POOL
4 TENNIS COURT
5 TENNIS COURT SEATING AREA
6 PAINTING STORAGE
7 BATHROOM
8 OUTDOOR SHOWER

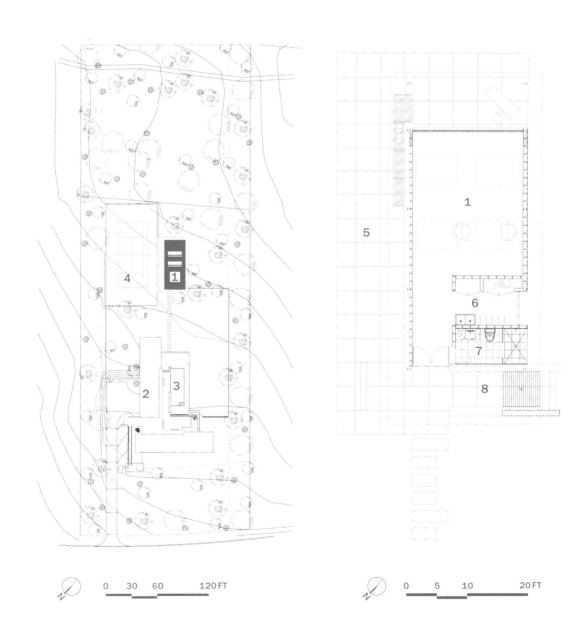

0   30   60   120 FT

0   5   10   20 FT

The main façade facing the
pool continues the material
of the pool deck

A wall of travertine conceals
an outdoor shower

The main room is one large space with clerestories and skylights.

On the south side a wall of glass with large sliding panels opens to a private terrace, providing a place for contemplation.

On the west side, facing the tennis court, a long blank stucco wall stretches out like a blank canvas

PARK AVENUE
RESIDENCE

LOCATION: **PARK AVENUE, CARNEGIE HILL NEIGHBORHOOD, NEW YORK CITY, NEW YORK, USA**
SITE: **14TH FLOOR APARTMENT**
TOTAL AREA: **2,800 SQUARE FEET**
PROGRAM: **3 BEDROOMS, 3 BATHROOMS, LIVING ROOM, DINING ROOM, FAMILY/MEDIA ROOM, STUDY/GUESTROOM, KITCHEN AND EAT-IN AREA**
STATUS: **COMPLETED 2006**

This Park Avenue project is a gut renovation of a 2,800-square-foot apartment located in a prewar building in the desirable Carnegie Hill neighborhood of Manhattan.

The architecture creates a state of equilibrium by juxtaposing the traditional classical layout of a prewar apartment with the openness of modernism.

Upon entering the apartment, a long, wide gallery stretches from north to south and connects different parts of the apartment. All private bedroom spaces are along the west wall of this gallery and are marked by monumental dark wenge wood doors with floor-to-ceiling frames, not only defining the entrance to the private spaces behind but also offering rhythm and movement moving forward toward the living space. A vestibule behind a translucent screen and defined by a "folded plane" (all in wenge wood) becomes a transitional space before entering the living space. This vestibule connects the public spaces of the apartment such as living, dining, library, study, and kitchen. The modernist ideology of living is expressed through the concept of layering, continuity, and transparency of space.

The living, dining, and library space all connect and separate through layers of translucent walls and sliding panels, allowing natural light to penetrate to all the spaces from east to west and creating the flexibility to entertain small intimate groups with the ability to expand the space for larger events and gatherings.

The careful selection of materials and furnishings offers a sense of luxury and refinement, while the quiet, solitary composition and layering of space simultaneously offers a stark and monastic experience. Conceptually, it is exactly this experience of living between complementary opposites that is the driving force behind the design of this project.

1 ENTRY/GALLERY
2 LIVING ROOM
3 DINING ROOM
4 LIBRARY/MEDIA ROOM
5 STUDY/GUEST ROOM
6 KITCHEN
7 BEDROOM
8 MASTER BEDROOM

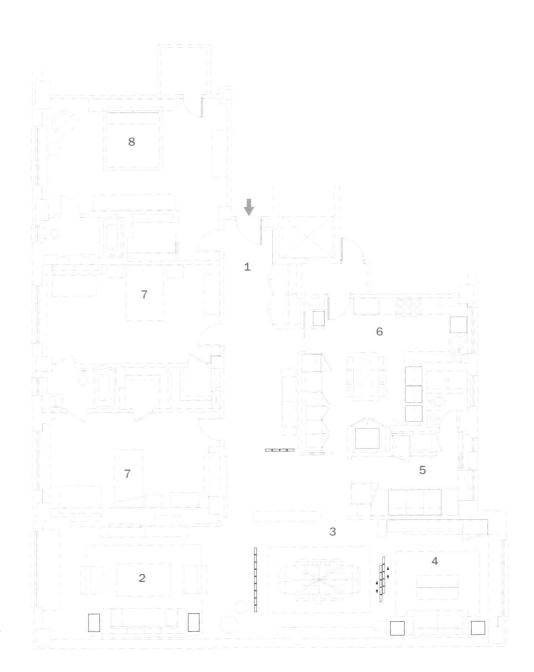

0   3   6   12 FT

The living, dining, and library spaces all
connect and separate through layers of
translucent walls and sliding panels

220

The modernist ideology of living is
expressed through the concept of
layering, continuity, and transparency
of space

The sliding panels create flexibility to entertain small intimate groups with the ability to expand space for larger events and gatherings

The careful selection of
materials and furnishings
offers a sense of luxury and
refinement

SAGAPONAC HOUSE

2004

CLIENT: **HARRY (COCO) BROWN II, BROWN COMPANY DEVELOMENT**
LOCATION: **EAST HAMPTON, LONG ISLAND, NEW YORK, USA**
SITE: **100-ACRE DEVELOPMENT**
TOTAL LOT AREA: **2.7 ACRES**
TOTAL HOUSE AREA: **5,000 SQUARE FEET**
PROGRAM: **4 BEDROOMS, 4 BATHROOMS, HOME OFFICE, FAMILY/TV AREA, OPEN KITCHEN, DINING, LIVING, LIBRARY, SCREENING ROOM, GYM, POOL, TENNIS COURT AND PAINTING STUDIO ADDED IN 2006**
STATUS: **COMPLETED 2004**

This 5,000-square-foot house sits on 2.7 acres of wooded land in the middle of potato fields between the fashionable South and East Hampton areas of Long Island, New York. The spatial configuration of this speculative house invites a variety of personalities and occupants, from reclusive individuals to sociable couples and groups, to be "original" and invent their own way of habitation in this structure.

In contrast to most oversized showplaces, suburban 'McMansions', and overstated country houses, this house is composed of two simple rectangular volumes forming an L-shaped plan. It frames and engages the landscape and the pleasures of being in the country. The center of the house is the main public space, with a swimming pool, multi-level terraces, and a covered porch with a shower. This space is accessible and visible from all other parts of the house, and at times it is visible to the neighbors and the street, becoming a stage for action and display. This private pool area, similar to some beaches in the area, becomes a stage for exhibitionism and spectatorship.

Inspired by Giacometti's sculpture, *Figure in a Box Between Two Boxes which are Houses*, the Sagaponac House takes the form of a minimalist structure placed on a platform within an untouched natural landscape.

A large opening within each rectangular volume frames the private life within the house and the pool beyond. These openings appear and disappear via a system of metal shutters mounted on the exterior walls, investigating the cultural definition of the domestic enclosure. These metal shutters not only act as a shield against intruders when no one is at home, they also reveal and conceal private and public hidden motivations, social interactions, and exchanges within and beyond the house.

1 SAGAPONAC HOUSE
2 POOL
3 TENNIS COURT
4 PAINTING STUDIO
5 ENTRY
6 DINING
7 KITCHEN
8 FAMILY/TV ROOM
9 MASTER BEDROOM
10 GUEST SUITE
11 LIVING ROOM
12 BEDROOM

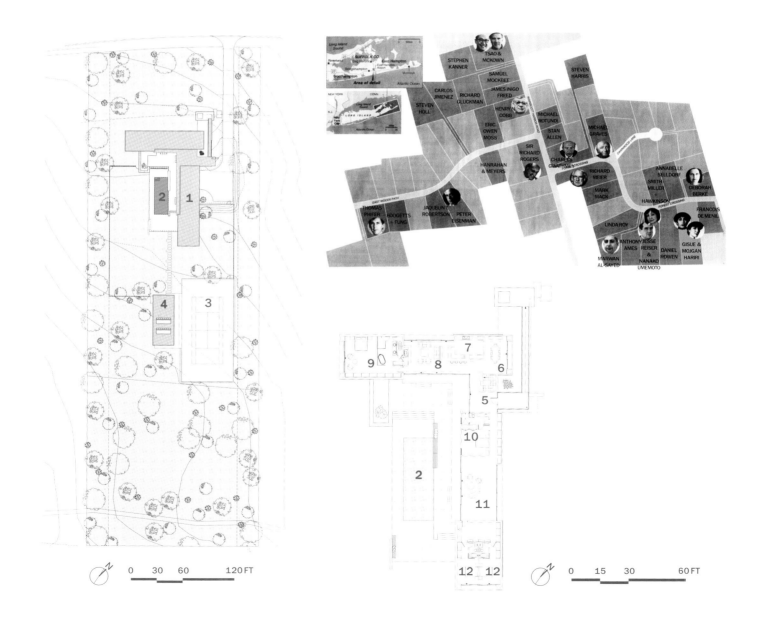

0 30 60   120 FT

0 15 30   60 FT

Inspired by Giacometti's sculpture, *Figure in a Box Between Two Boxes Which are Houses*, the Sagaponac House takes the form of a minimalist structure placed on a platform within an untouched natural landscape

A large opening in each rectangular volume frames the private life in the house and becomes a stage for exhibitionism and spectatorship. Here one can display to the public one's private voyeurism and desires.

ART LIGHTING FURNITURE

SWAROVSKI CHANDELIER

2006

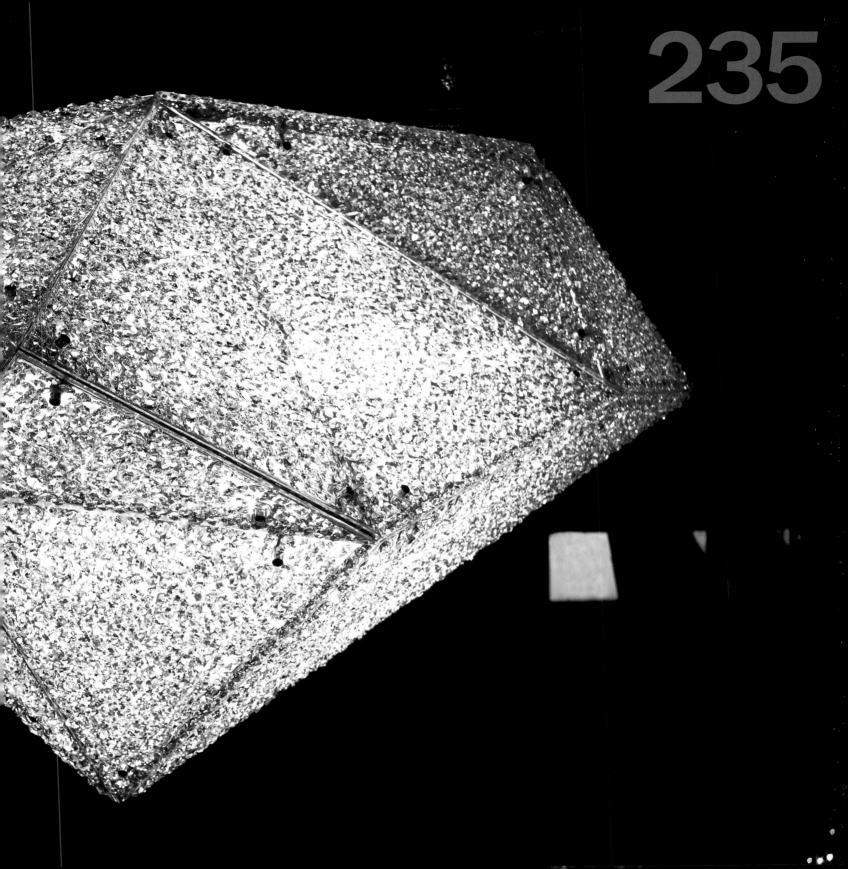

CLIENT: **SWAROVSKI**
DIMENSIONS: **7 FEET 6 INCHES BY 3 FEET 6 INCHES BY 3 FEET 6 INCHES**
SERIES: **CRYSTAL PALACE COLLECTION**
EXHIBITED: **ART BASEL, MIAMI BEACH, USA, 2006;**
THE SALONE INTERNAZIONALE DEL MOBILE, MILAN, ITALY, 2007

The geometry of this chandelier
follows the geological formations
and cutting of precious stones
with very sharp edges, folds and
multiple points

Swarovski's commitment to reinvent the chandelier to suit contemporary culture and residential environments encouraged us to examine the history and qualities of crystals and chandeliers.

What is most striking about all chandeliers—traditional or modern—is their ability to create a vibrant and sparkling atmosphere. Their design is an armature to hang the crystals from. We wanted to reverse this notion and fundamentally create the crystal itself. We were interested in making the diamond, not the ring.

World-class craftsmanship, technical innovation, and the beauty of Swarovski crystals inspired and encouraged the concept and formation of this fixture.

After being fascinated by the variety of Swarovski crystals we decided to take the idea of the cut stone as the essence of Swarovski and make that the concept of our chandelier. It is because of this concept that we have named our chandelier ROCK CRYSTAL, as its geometry follows the geological formations and cutting of precious stones with very sharp edges, folds, and multiple points. The form of this crystal-shaped chandelier is asymmetrical and varies from different angles and points of view.

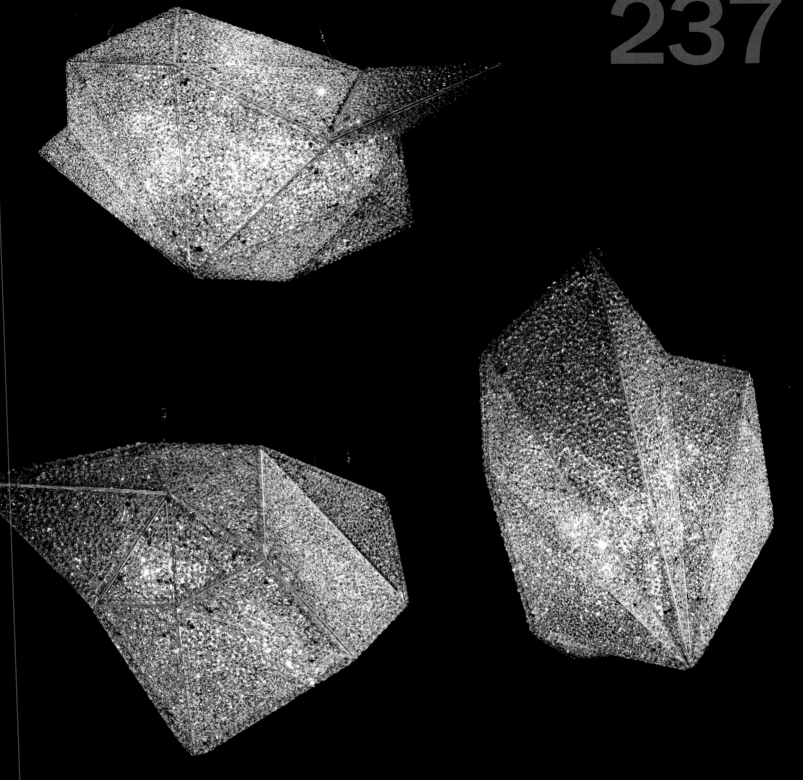

DIGITAL GEAR

2003–2005

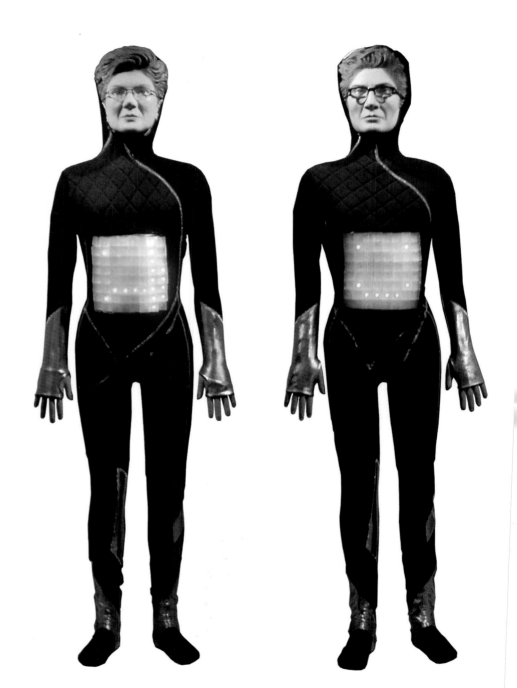

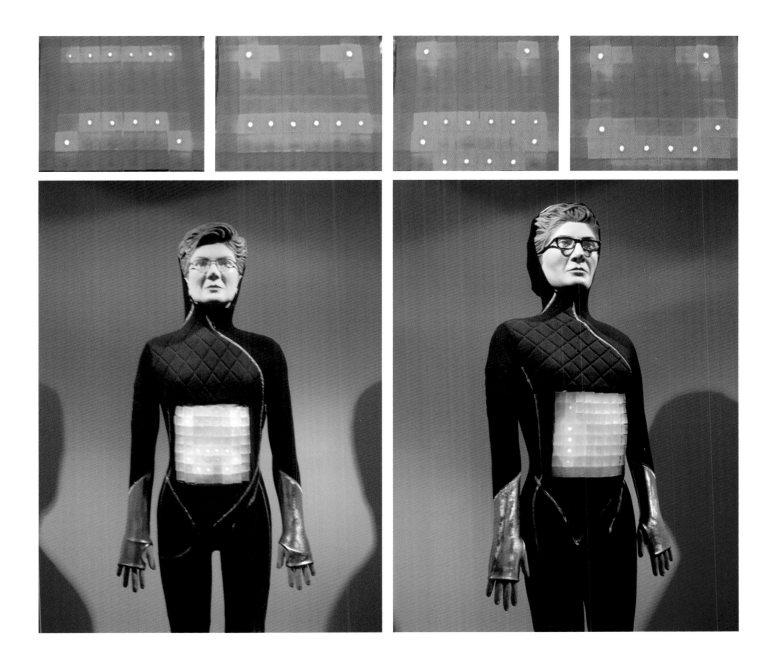

"The meaning of clothing in contemporary culture was at the heart of *Dressing Ourselves*, an art exhibition curated by Italian architect and designer Alessandro Guerriero. Do clothes really represent our way of thinking and our lifestyle? Are they an expression of our true self? These are just a few of the questions Guerriero posed with the exhibition.

Guerriero asked 30 internationally acclaimed architects and artists to create 'self-portraits' in the form of clothes displayed on life-size statues of the artists. The surprising results blended a variety of disciplines, including art, technology, industrial design, architecture and fashion, and are a testament to Guerriero's strong belief in individualism and the uniqueness of the mind. The clothes and the statues were displayed at Milan's Triennale Design Museum in January 2005.

The exhibition was sponsored and promoted by Yoox.com, the Bologna-based discount designer fashion retailer that describes itself as an 'E-concept' store—similar to Paris' Colette, only online.

The exhibition then moved to other cities, including New York, London, Paris, and Tokyo."

Luisa Zargani, *Women's Wear Daily*, November 10, 2004

Similar to our Digital–House prototype, this Digital Gear facilitates communication and connection to our global culture. It is clothing of the 21st century. The body suit is made of a material that has a grid of LED lights woven into it, which are powered by a layer of paper batteries and can be activated to reveal your inner emotions through the language of emoticons.

Emoticons are used by the digital generation to compensate for the inability to convey voice inflections, facial expressions, and bodily gestures in written communication. Emoticons are an effective tool for avoiding misinterpretation of intentions. They are about speed and precision in communication.

We speak different languages and yet we interact, communicate and participate in a conversation. Who we are is what we wear, what we feel, and what we can potentially say.

hm, maybe... (being indifferent)

wink

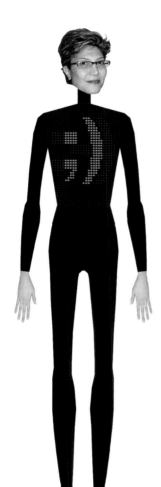

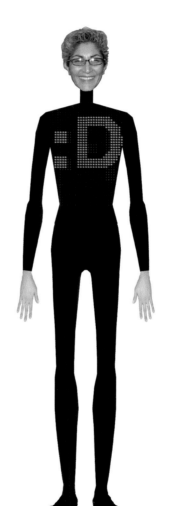

that's so funny! (laughing)

oh, how surprised I am!

RYOANJI TABLE COLLECTION

1992

In these tables, industrial bar grating is used to evoke the traditional Japanese Zen garden. "The linear repetition of bars and the stillness created by the placement of objects on the grating reminded us of the Ryoanji gardens."

The collection embodies the belief that architecture goes beyond utilitarian needs; that in some way it is possible to stretch the perception of the mundane and, in doing so, evoke alternative meaning.

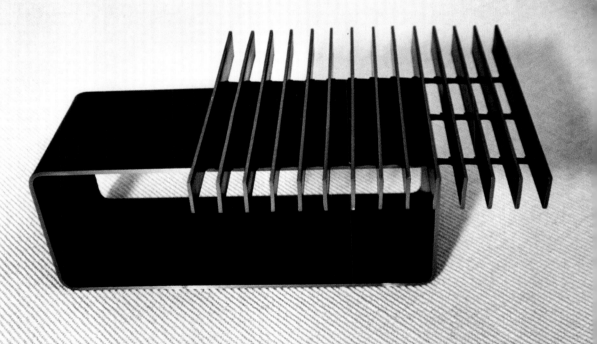

CLOUD LIGHT COLLECTION

1992

All the works in the collection are hand formed, which makes each piece unique and different. The cloud lights in the collection are sculpted and stitched by hand so that each becomes an exceptional work in its own right.

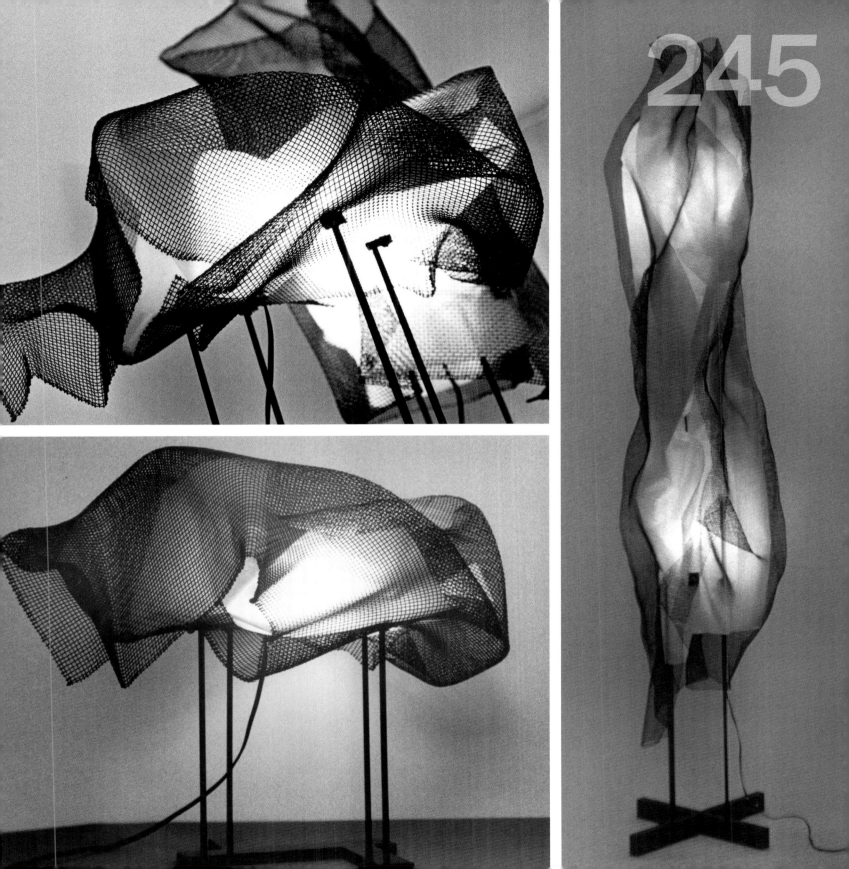

STASIS LIGHT
COLLECTION

1986

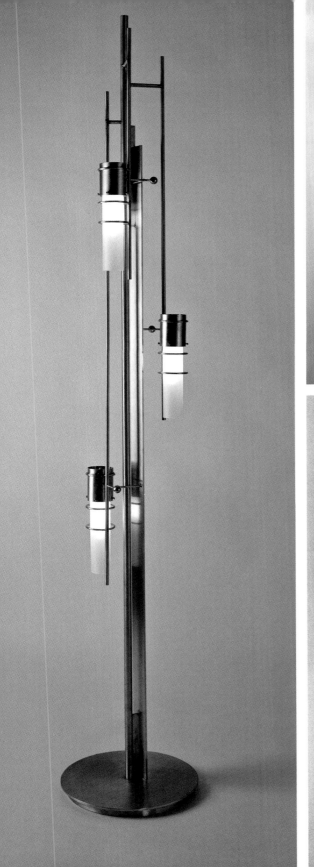

Hariri and Hariri have been designing furniture and lighting since 1986 as one of a kind pieces for their architectural projects. Their furniture, like their architecture, investigates the nature of materials through inventive geometric form.

In this collection they have chosen to work primarily with metal and glass—juxtaposing materials of industry, such as carbon steel bar grating or wire mesh, with materials of opacity, such as sandblasted glass or fiberglass cloth. It is this unexpected combination of materials that gives the pieces an "industrial elegance".

GALILEO STOOL

1992

SOLARIS STOOL

1986

CREDITS

SALZBURG RESIDENTIAL COMPLEX
CLIENT: ERNST SCHOLDAN/
ASSET ONE IMMOBILIENENTWICKLUNGS AG
ARCHITECT: HARIRI & HARIRI – ARCHITECTURE
DESIGN TEAM: GISUE HARIRI, MOJGAN HARIRI,
MARKUS RANDLER, THIERRY PFISTER, JENNY
SHOUKIMAS, LIV MARIT NAESS, MARLENE KWEE,
NEDA POURSHAKOURI
SALZBURG TEAM: KLEBOTH.LINDINGER.ARCHITECTEN
ZT-KEG, ARINCO PLANUNGS+CONSULTING GMBH
STRUCTURAL ENGINEER: HERBRICH CONSULT
MEP ENGINEER: TECHNISCHES BÜRO EDHOFER,
PLANUNGSBÜRO EDELMANN
LANDSCAPE DESIGNER: KARIN STANDLER
RENDERINGS & PHOTOS:
HARIRI & HARIRI – ARCHITECTURE

THE HIGHLINE COMMUNITY
CLIENT: FRIENDS OF THE HIGHLINE
ARCHITECT: HARIRI & HARIRI – ARCHITECTURE
DESIGN TEAM: GISUE HARIRI, MOJGAN HARIRI,
THIERRY PFISTER, MARKUS RANDLER
RENDERINGS: HARIRI & HARIRI – ARCHITECTURE

CANADIAN COPTIC VILLAGE
CLIENT: ST. MARK'S COPTIC CHRISTIAN ORTHODOX
CHURCH (MARKHAM, ONTARIO, CANADA)
ARCHITECT: HARIRI & HARIRI – ARCHITECTURE
DESIGN TEAM: GISUE HARIRI, MOJGAN HARIRI,
THIERRY PFISTER, MARKUS RANDLER
STRUCTURAL ENGINEER: ROBERT SILMAN
ASSOCIATES, P.C.
RENDERINGS: HARIRI & HARIRI – ARCHITECTURE

DALLAS LOFT BUILDING
CLIENT: BILLINGSLEY DEVELOPMENT COMPANY
ARCHITECT: HARIRI & HARIRI – ARCHITECTURE
DESIGN TEAM: GISUE HARIRI, MOJGAN HARIRI,
MARKUS RANDLER, JENNY SHOUKIMAS, NICO KAFI
DALLAS TEAM:
PROJECT MANAGER: LUCILO PEÑA
ARCHITECT OF RECORD: HENSLEY LAMKIN RACHEL, INC.
STRUCTURAL ENGINEER: BROCKETTE/DAVIS/DRAKE, INC.
MEP ENGINEER: BLUM CONSULTING ENGINEERS, INC.
LIGHTING DESIGNER: SCOTT OLDNER LIGHTING
DESIGN, LLC
LANDSCAPE DESIGNER: MESA
RENDERINGS: HARIRI & HARIRI – ARCHITECTURE &
BILLINGSLEY COMPANY

SOUTH STREET TOWER
CLIENT: ANBAU ENTERPRISES, INC.
ARCHITECT: HARIRI & HARIRI – ARCHITECTURE
DESIGN TEAM: GISUE HARIRI, MOJGAN HARIRI,
MARKUS RANDLER, JENNY SHOUKIMAS
STRUCTURAL ENGINEER: ROBERT SILMAN
ASSOCIATES, P.C.
MEP ENGINEER: IP GROUP
LIGHTING DESIGNER: HORTON LEES BROGDEN
LIGHTING DESIGN
LEED CONSULTANT: COMMUNITY ENVIRONMENTAL
CENTER
RENDERINGS: HARIRI & HARIRI – ARCHITECTURE &
PAUL DOMZAL

WTC WEEPING TOWERS
ARCHITECT: HARIRI & HARIRI – ARCHITECTURE
DESIGN TEAM: GISUE HARIRI, MOJGAN HARIRI,
JAIME OLIVER, MARKUS RANDLER, NACK LEE
RENDERINGS: HARIRI & HARIRI – ARCHITECTURE

PRIVATE EQUITY OFFICES
ARCHITECTURE & INTERIOR DESIGN:
HARIRI & HARIRI – ARCHITECTURE
DESIGN TEAM: GISUE HARIRI, MOJGAN HARIRI,
AARON MCDONALD, JENNY SHOUKIMAS,
MARLENE KWEE, MARKUS RANDLER
STRUCTURAL ENGINEER: ROBERT SILMAN
ASSOCIATES, P.C.
MEP ENGINEER: IP GROUP
GENERAL CONTRACTOR: STRUCTURE TONE
LIGHTING CONSULTANT: HORTON LEES BROGDEN
LIGHTING DESIGN
PHOTOGRAPHY: PAUL WARCHOL

UNIFIED FIELD OFFICES
CLIENT: UNIFIED FIELD
ARCHITECT: HARIRI & HARIRI – ARCHITECTURE
DESIGN TEAM: GISUE HARIRI, MOJGAN HARIRI,
CHARLES JORDAN, PHILIPPE LE ROY, MASON WHITE
STRUCTURAL ENGINEER: ROBERT SILMAN
ASSOCIATES, P.C.
METALWORK: KERN ROCKENFIELD INC.
PHOTOGRAPHY: EDUARD HUEBER

EPI CENTER MALL PROTOTYPE
CLIENT: GORDON/BRANT LLP
ARCHITECT: HARIRI & HARIRI – ARCHITECTURE
DESIGN TEAM: GISUE HARIRI, MOJGAN HARIRI,
THIERRY PFISTER, MICHAEL TOWER
RENDERINGS: HARIRI & HARIRI – ARCHITECTURE

ISSEY MIYAKE TRIBECA
CLIENT: ISSEY MIYAKE
ARCHITECT: HARIRI & HARIRI – ARCHITECTURE
DESIGN TEAM: GISUE HARIRI, MOJGAN HARIRI,
THIERRY PFISTER, MASON WHITE
RENDERINGS: HARIRI & HARIRI – ARCHITECTURE

TUI PRANICH SHOWROOM
CLIENT: TUI PRANICH
ARCHITECT: HARIRI & HARIRI – ARCHITECTURE
DESIGN TEAM: GISUE HARIRI, MOJGAN HARIRI
PHOTOGRAPHY: THOMAS LOOF

JSM MUSIC STUDIOS
CLIENT: JSM MUSIC
ARCHITECT: HARIRI & HARIRI – ARCHITECTURE
DESIGN TEAM: GISUE HARIRI, MOJGAN HARIRI,
PAUL BAIRD
STRUCTURAL ENGINEER: ROBERT SILMAN
ASSOCIATES, P.C.
PHOTOGRAPHY: PAUL WARCHOL

MUSEUM OF 21ST CENTURY
CLIENT: THE PARKER GROUP—DEVELOPERS
ARCHITECT: HARIRI & HARIRI – ARCHITECTURE
DESIGN TEAM: GISUE HARIRI, MOJGAN HARIRI,
THIERRY PFISTER, MARKUS RANDLER
RENDERINGS: HARIRI & HARIRI – ARCHITECTURE

ROCA NEW YORK
CLIENT: ROCKLAND CENTER FOR THE ARTS
ARCHITECT: HARIRI & HARIRI — ARCHITECTURE
DESIGN TEAM: GISUE HARIRI, MOJGAN HARIRI,
THIERRY PFISTER, MARKUS RANDLER,
MASON WHITE, SILVIA SOKALSKI, AARON
MCDONALD, MARLENE KWEE
STRUCTURAL ENGINEER: ROBERT SILMAN
ASSOCIATES, P.C.
MEP ENGINEER: IP GROUP
RENDERINGS: HARIRI & HARIRI — ARCHITECTURE

CINE FILM CENTER
CLIENT: TRIBECA FILM FESTIVAL,
CONGLOMERATE OF PRIVATE PRODUCTION
COMPANIES AND THE CITY OF NEW YORK
ARCHITECT: HARIRI & HARIRI — ARCHITECTURE
DESIGN TEAM: GISUE HARIRI, MOJGAN HARIRI
RENDERINGS: HARIRI & HARIRI — ARCHITECTURE

KOMA LOS ANGELES
CLIENT: KOMA, PLUS OF KOREA
ARCHITECT: HARIRI & HARIRI — ARCHITECTURE
DESIGN TEAM: GISUE HARIRI, MOJGAN HARIRI,
THIERRY PFISTER, ANNE UHLMANN, PAUL BAIRD,
PHILIPPE LE ROY
RENDERINGS: HARIRI & HARIRI — ARCHITECTURE

HIGH LINE HOTEL
CLIENT: BISHOPSCOURT REALTY, LLC
ARCHITECT: HARIRI & HARIRI — ARCHITECTURE
DESIGN TEAM: GISUE HARIRI, MOJGAN HARIRI,
JENNY SHOUKIMAS
RENDERINGS: HARIRI & HARIRI — ARCHITECTURE

HOTEL DUBAI
CLIENT: ADNAN AL—MAIMANI
ARCHITECT: HARIRI & HARIRI — ARCHITECTURE
DESIGN TEAM: GISUE HARIRI, MOJGAN HARIRI,
THIERRY PFISTER, JENNY SHOUKIMAS,
MARLENE KWEE, NEDA POURSHAKOURI
RENDERINGS: HARIRI & HARIRI — ARCHITECTURE

JUAN VALDEZ FLAGSHIP
CLIENT: NATIONAL FEDERATION OF COLOMBIAN
COFFEE GROWERS
ARCHITECT: HARIRI & HARIRI — ARCHITECTURE
DESIGN TEAM: GISUE HARIRI, MOJGAN HARIRI,
MARKUS RANDLER, THIERRY PFISTER
COLOMBIAN TEAM: RIR ARQUITECTOS/
JUAN CARLOS ROJAS
MEP ENGINEER: IP GROUP
STRUCTURAL ENGINEER: ROBERT SILMAN
ASSOCIATES, P.C.
LIGHTING CONSULTANT: HORTON LEES BROGDEN
LIGHTING DESIGN
GENERAL CONTRATOR: RICHTER + RATNER
PHOTOGRAPHY: PAUL WARCHOL

TUTTLE STREET RESTAURANT
CLIENT: DACRA/CRAIG ROBINS
ARCHITECT: HARIRI & HARIRI — ARCHITECTURE
DESIGN TEAM: GISUE HARIRI, MOJGAN HARIRI,
MARKUS RANDLER
RENDERINGS: HARIRI & HARIRI — ARCHITECTURE

SUTTON PLACE RESIDENCE
CLIENT: KAMBIZ & NAZGOL SHAHBAZI
ARCHITECTURE & INTERIOR DESIGN:
HARIRI & HARIRI — ARCHITECTURE
DESIGN TEAM: GISUE HARIRI, MOJGAN HARIRI,
THIERRY PFISTER, BIEINNA HAM
MEP ENGINEERS: IP GROUP CONSULTING ENGINEERS
LIGHTING CONSULTANT: LIGHTING WORKSHOP
GENERAL CONTRACTOR: J & J JOHNSON
AUDIO-VISUAL CONSULTANT: DCM SYSTEMS
PHOTOGRAPHY: PAUL WARCHOL

WILTON POOLHOUSE
CLIENT: KAMBIZ & NAZGOL SHAHBAZI
ARCHITECT: HARIRI & HARIRI — ARCHITECTURE
DESIGN TEAM: GISUE HARIRI, MOJGAN HARIRI,
MARKUS RANDLER
STRUCTURAL ENGINEER: ROBERT SILMAN
ASSOCIATES, P.C.
SURVEYOR: RYAN AND FAULDS, LLC.
GENERAL CONTRACTOR: WILLOW WOODWORKING
PHOTOGRAPHY: PAUL WARCHOL

SAGAPONAC PAINTING STUDIO
CLIENT: HOWARD LAZAR
ARCHITECT: HARIRI & HARIRI — ARCHITECTURE
DESIGN TEAM: GISUE HARIRI, MOJGAN HARIRI,
MARKUS RANDLER
STRUCTURAL ENGINEER: ROBERT SILMAN &
ASSOCIATES, P.C.
SURVEYOR: BARYLSKI LAND SURVEYOR, P.C.
GENERAL CONTRACTOR: RONAN O'DWYER
PHOTOGRAPHY: PAUL WARCHOL

PARK AVENUE RESIDENCE
CLIENT: DENNIS & JANET PAGE
ARCHITECTURE & INTERIOR DESIGN:
HARIRI & HARIRI — ARCHITECTURE
DESIGN TEAM: GISUE HARIRI, MOJGAN HARIRI,
THIERRY PFISTER
MEP ENGINEER: IP GROUP
AUDIO-VISUAL CONSULTANT: DCM SYSTEMS
GENERAL CONTRACTOR: BERNSOHN & FETNER, LLC
PHOTOGRAPHY: PAUL WARCHOL

SAGAPONAC HOUSE
CLIENT: HARRY "COCO" BROWN
ARCHITECT: HARIRI & HARIRI — ARCHITECTURE
DESIGN TEAM: GISUE HARIRI, MOJGAN HARIRI,
THIERRY PFISTER, MARKUS RANDLER
STRUCTURAL ENGINEER: ROBERT SILMAN &
ASSOCIATES, P.C.
SURVEYOR: BARYLSKI LAND SURVEYOR, P.C.
GENERAL CONTRACTOR: RONAN O'DWYER
PHOTOGRAPHY: PAUL WARCHOL, JEAN-FRANCOIS
JAUSSAUD

SWAROVSKI CHANDELIER
CLIENT: NADJA SWAROVSKI
DESIGNER: HARIRI & HARIRI — ARCHITECTURE
DESIGN TEAM: GISUE HARIRI, MOJGAN HARIRI,
MARKUS RANDLER
RENDERINGS: HARIRI & HARIRI — ARCHITECTURE
PHOTOS COURTESY OF SWAROVSKI CRYSTAL
PALACE

DIGITAL GEAR
CLIENT: ALESSANDRO GUERRIERO & YOOX.COM
DESIGNER: HARIRI & HARIRI — ARCHITECTURE
DESIGN TEAM: GISUE HARIRI, MOJGAN HARIRI,
MARKUS RANDLER
TECHNOLOGY: JAMES CLAR

RYOANJI TABLE COLLECTION
STASIS LIGHT COLLECTION
DESIGN: HARIRI & HARIRI — ARCHITECTURE
MANUFACTURE: GEORGE KOVACS

CLOUD LIGHT COLLECTION
GALILEO STOOL
SOLARIS STOOL
DESIGN: HARIRI & HARIRI — ARCHITECTURE
PRODUCTION: H+3 INC. (LIMITED EDITION)

BIBLIOGRAPHY

MONOGRAPHS

"HARIRI & HARIRI HOUSES", RIZZOLI INTERNATIONAL, NEW YORK, 2005.

RIERA OJEDA, OSCAR, "HARIRI & HARIRI" IN CASAS INTERNATIONAL 48. KLICZKOWSKI, ARGENTINA, APRIL 1997.

HARIRI & HARIRI, "WORK IN PROGRESS", THE MONACELLI PRESS, NEW YORK, 1995.

BOOKS

GALINDO, MICHELLE, "1000 X ARCHITECTURE OF THE AMERICAS", VERLAGSHAUS BRAUN, GERMANY, 2008, PP. 151, 213.

RIHAN, XING, TIANBIN, LI, "100 X 400", H.K. RIHAN INT'L CULTURE SPREAD LIMITED, HONG KING, 2008. PP. 440–447.

TSANG, DIANE, "HOME", PACE PUBLISHING LIMITED, HONG KONG, 2008. PP. 62–73.

PUGLISI, LUIGI PRESTINENZA, "NEW DIRECTIONS IN CONTEMPORARY ARCHITECTURE: EVOLUTIONS AND REVOLUTIONS IN BUILDING DESIGN SINCE 1988", JOHN WILEY & SONS, LTD, ITALY, 2008, PP. 135–138.

MCCULLOCH, JANELLE, "VIEW FROM THE TOP: GRAND APARTMENT LIVING", THE IMAGES PUBLISHING GROUP PTY LTD, AUSTRALIA, 2008, PP. 54–59.

YEUNG, YAN, "RESTAURANT", PACE PUBLISHING, HONG KONG, 2007, PP. 108–115.

ZEC, PETER, "WHO'S WHO IN DESIGN – THE LEADING DESIGNERS OF THE WORLD VOL. 3", RED DOT EDITION, ESSEN, 2007, PP. 346–347.

KUHN, CHRISTIAN, "STERNBRAUEREI SITE REDEVELOPMENT COMPETITION", VERLAG ANTON PUSTET, AUSTRIA, 2007, PP. 67–73.

ISHERWOOD, BOB & MYERS, RICHARD, "WORLD CHANGING IDEAS", PALAZZO EDITIONS LTD, BATH, 2006, P. 117.

GENGHINI, MATTEO & SOLOMITA, PASQUALINO, "LOFT 2", MOTTA ARCHITETTURA, MILAN, 2007, PP. 178–185.

GENGHINI, MATTEO & SOLOMITA, PASQUALINO, "CAFFÈ E RISTORANTI 2", MOTTA ARCHITETTURA, MILAN, 2007, PP. 172-181.

GLOBAL INTERIOR DESIGN COLLECTION, "JUAN VALDEZ FLAGSHIP CAFÉ NEW YORK", PP. 108–111.

HASANOVIC, AISHA, "2000 ARCHITECTS", THE IMAGES PUBLISHING GROUP, AUSTRALIA, 2006, P. 270.

VERCELLONI, MATTEO, "LOFTS & APARTMENTS IN NYC 2", EDIZIONI L'ARCHIVOLTO, 2006, PP. 94–109.

SUEYOSHI, HIROKO, "JUAN VALDEZ FLAGSHIP CAFÉ NY" IN SPA-DE, VOL. 3, 2005, PP. 38–41.

GUERRIERO, ALESSANDRO, "DRESSING OURSELVES", EDIZIONI CHARTA, 2005, PP. 52–53.

RESCHKE, CYNTHIA, "PACIFIC HOUSES", HARPER DESIGN INTERNATIONAL, 2004. PP. 156–163.

BROWN, HARRY J., "AMERICAN DREAM: THE HOUSES AT SAGAPONAC", RIZZOLI INTERNATIONAL, 2003, PP. 96–103.

CHRISTIAANSE KEES, HANS IBELINGS A.O. STRIP, "ONE MILE OF URBAN PLANNING IN THE HAGUE", NAI PUBLISHERS, 2003.

"OFFICE SPACES – A PICTORIAL REVIEW", THE IMAGES PUBLISHING GROUP, AUSTRALIA, 2003, PP. 24–25.

PROTETCH, MAX, STUART KRIMKO, "A NEW WORLD TRADE CENTER: DESIGN PROPOSALS FROM LEADING ARCHITECTS WORLDWIDE", REGAN BOOKS, 2002, PP. 60–61.

TOY, MAGGIE, "THE ARCHITECT – WOMEN IN CONTEMPORARY ARCHITECTURE", IMAGES PUBLISHING GROUP, AUSTALIA, 2001, PP. 74–79.

GRAYSON TRULOVE, JAMES AND KIM, IL, "THE NEW AMERICAN HOUSE 3", WHITNEY LIBRARY OF DESIGN, 2001, PP. 112–119.

LANG HO, CATHY, AND RAUL A. BARRENECHE, "HOUSE: AMERICAN HOUSES FOR THE NEW CENTURY", NEW YORK: UNIVERSE PUBLISHING, 2001.

RICHARDS, IVOR, "MANHATTAN LOFTS", JOHN WILEY & SONS, LONDON, 2000, PP. 86–95.

ASENSIO, PACO, "MOUNTAIN HOUSES", HARPERCOLLINS, NEW YORK, 2000, PP. 34–41.

MOSTADI, ARIAN, "THE AMERICAN HOUSE TODAY", ARCHITECTURE SHOWCASE, BARCELONA, SPAIN, 2000, PP. 136–145.

RILEY, TERENCE, "THE UN-PRIVATE HOUSE", MUSEUM OF MODERN ART, NEW YORK, 1999, PP. 56–59.

SMITH BROWNSTEIN, ELIZABETH, "IF THIS HOUSE COULD TALK…", SIMON & SCHUSTER, NEW YORK, 1999, PP. 240–247.

DOUBILET, SUSAN, AND DARALICE BOLES, "BARRY'S BAY COTTAGE" IN AMERICAN HOUSE NOW, UNIVERSE, NEW YORK, 1997, PP. 36–43.

SIREFMAN, SUSANNA, "NEW YORK – A GUIDE TO RECENT ARCHITECTURE", ELLIPIS KONEMANN, 1997, PP. 98–99.

RIERA OJEDA, OSCAR, "THE NEW AMERICAN HOUSE", WHITNEY LIBRARY OF DESIGN, NEW YORK, 1995, PP. 212–219.

RUSSEL, BEVERLY, "40 UNDER 40 – A GUIDE TO NEW YOUNG TALENTS WITH SEDUCTIVE IDEAS FOR LIVING TODAY", VITAE PUBLISHING, INC., 1995, PP. 152–163.

PHILLIPS, PATRICIA, "BEARINGS" IN PRINCETON ARCHITECTURAL PRESS, PARSONS SCHOOL OF DESIGN, EXHIBITION CATALOGUE, 1988–89, PP. 30–33.

PERIODICALS

"THE UN-PRIVATE APARTMENT" IN INTERIOR DESIGN, MARCH 2009, PP. 218–225.

"STUDIO VISIT – HARIRI & HARIRI ARCHITECTURE" IN THE ARCHITECT'S NEWSPAPER, DEC. 10, 2008, PP. 16–17.

"LIGHT AS AIR" IN INTERIOR DESIGN, SEPTEMBER 2008, PP. 282–287.

"VISION QUEST" IN HAMPTONS COTTAGES AND GARDENS, JULY 15–31 2008, P70–75.

"IN THE FRAME" IN CONNECTICUT COTTAGES & GARDENS, JULY 2008, PP. 80–85.

BEAUTYMAN, MAIRI, "STERNBRAUEREI, SALZBURG, AUSTRIA" IN ROBBREPORT VACATION HOMES, FEBRUARY/MARCH 2008, PP. 44–45.

GIOVANNI, JOSEPH, "CREATIVE REFLECTIONS" IN ARCHITECTURAL DIGEST, MAY 2008, PP. 248–259.

THURMAN, JUDITH, "MINIMALIST IN MANHATTAN" IN ARCHITECTURAL DIGEST, OCTOBER 2007, PP. 264–269.

"HARIRI SISTERS TAKE SALZBURG" IN ARCHITECTURAL RECORD, NOVEMBER 2006, P. 34.

"DIGITAL GEAR – BODY LANGUAGE-SUIT" IN TASARIM 164, SEPTEMBER 2006, PP. 20–22.

"A VICTORY FOR HARIRI & HARIRI" IN THE ARCHITECTS NEWSPAPER, SEPTEMBER 11, 2006, P. 12.

MCKEOUGH, TIM, "HARIRI SQUARED" IN CITY, MAY/JUNE 2006, PP. 56–59.

"PAGINE MINIMALISTE" IN ARCHITECTURAL DIGEST (ITALY), MAY 2006, P. 108.

KELLOG, CRAIG, "HALL OF FAME" IN INTERIOR DESIGN, DECEMBER 2005, PP. 8–10.

"HARIRI & HARIRI – ARCHITECTURE" IN ME'MAR, 33, OCTOBER/NOVEMBER 2005, PP. 64–71.

STEGNER, PETER, "LIQUID WALLS. CAFÉ 'JUAN VALDEZ' IN NEW YORK" IN BAUMEISTER, B9 2005, PP. 50–54.

FRIES, ANA MARIA, "CASAS COMPACTAS EN UN BARRIO DE ESTRELLAS" IN AXXIS, NO. 149-2005, PP. 20–28.

"THE FIRST ANNUAL HOSPITALITY DESIGN AWARDS" IN HOSPITALITY DESIGN, JULY 2005, PP. 74–75.

GARDINER, VIRGINIA, "SEEING WHAT DEVELOPS" IN DWELL, JUNE 2005, PP. 130–135.

MOSELEY, AMANDA, "READ ME" IN METROPOLIS, APRIL 2005, P. 42.

WEBB, MICHAEL, "PERKING UP" IN HOSPITALITY DESIGN, APRIL 2005, PP. 172–175.

VON WESTERSHEIMB, KAY, "GIACOMETTI ON LONG ISLAND" IN ARCHITEKTUR AKTUELL, APRIL 2005, PP. 120–127.

WETTSTEIN, KAY, "NOW IT'S SHOWTIME" IN WOHN!DESIGN, MARCH/APRIL 2005, PP. 58–68.

SFORNI, JASMINE, "DRESSED TO THRILL" IN SURFACE, NO. 52, P. 86.

MAKOVSKY, PAUL, AND ANDREW YANG, "THE TWENTY-FIRST-CENTURY COFFEE SHOP" IN METROPOLIS, MARCH 2005, P. 118.

GOODBODY, BRIDGET, "HARIRI & HARIRI – ONE ON ONE" IN ART ASIA PACIFIC, NO. 42, PP. 34–36.

COLMAN, DAVID, "ON A CURVE" IN ELLE DECOR, MARCH 2005, PP. 102–107.

WEBB, MICHAEL, "CAFFEINE H(E)AVEN" IN FRAME, JANUARY/FEBRUARY 2005, P. 40.

ABRAMOVITCH, INGRID, "AMERICAN SCENE-THIS MONTH ON THE DESIGN BEAT" IN HOUSE & GARDEN, JANUARY 2005, P. 45.

SCHOENEMAN, DEBORAH, "GEMS OF THE OCEAN" IN NEW YORK MAGAZINE, NOVEMBER 15, 2004, P. 78.

FORD, JEN, "THE HOUSE OF TOMORROW" IN HARPER'S BAZAAR, OCTOBER 2004, PP. 192–193.

"JUAN VALDEZ CAFÉ" IN NEW YORK MAGAZINE, OCTOBER 18, 2004, P. 60.

LOUIE, ELAINE, "HOMAGE TO COFFEE" IN THE NEW YORK TIMES, OCTOBER 14, P. F3.

GOLDBERGER, PAUL, "HOMES OF THE STARS" IN THE NEW YORKER, SEPTEMBER 13, 2004, PP. 96–98.

TANASE, OANA, "HARIRI & HARIRI - DIGITAL TECTONICS" IN IGLOO, JULY–AUGUST 2004, PP. 22–27.

"MODERN DREAM" IN THE NEW YORK TIMES "HOMES" SECTION, JULY 2004, COVER AND P. 2.

"THE AD 100: THE WORLD'S TOP DESIGNERS + ARCHITECTS." ARCHITECTURAL DIGEST, JANUARY 2004, P. 80.

BERNSTEIN, FRED, "FROM INDUSTRIAL RELIC TO BRAVE NEW WORLD: THE HIGH LINE GETS A SECOND CHANCE" IN ARCHITECTURAL RECORD, OCTOBER 2003, PP. 73–74.

"TOP OF THE LINE" IN SURFACE, NO. 43, AUGUST 2003, PP. 162–170.

MELLINS, THOMAS, "THE GAP BETWEEN THE PROMISE AND PROTOTYPE" IN ARCHITECTURAL RECORD, JULY 2003, PP. 74–80.

GORDON, ALASTAIR, "37 WAYS OF LOOKING AT A HAMPTON" IN VANITY FAIR, MAY 2003, PP. 198–199.

LEISH BROWN, PATRICIA, "DOUBLE IDENTITY" IN ARCHITECTURAL DIGEST, MAY 2003, PP. 300–305.

GOODMAN, WENDY, "URBAN OASIS" IN NEW YORK MAGAZINE, OCTOBER 14, 2002, PP. 42–45.

RENZI, JEN, "SHOWING OFF" IN INTERIOR DESIGN, FEBRUARY 2002, PP. 188–190.

"HARIRI & HARIRI: ROCKLAND CENTER FOR THE ARTS." OCULUS, THE AMERICAN INSTITUTE OF ARCHITECTS, NEW YORK CHAPTER, VOL. 63, NO. 6, FEBRUARY 2001, P. 5.

FRANKEL, ELENA, "SPEAKING VOLUMES" IN INTERIOR DESIGN, VOL. 71, NO. 2, FEBRUARY 2000, PP. 146–153.

"FUTURES TO COME" IN ARCHITECTURAL RECORD, DECEMBER 1999, PP. 100–101.

BERNSTEIN, FRED, "RENOVATION" IN METROPOLITAN HOME, SEPTEMBER/OCTOBER 1999, PP. 163–171.

GOODMAN, WENDY, "HOME DESIGN 2000" IN NEW YORK MAGAZINE, OCTOBER 11, 1999, PP. 72–77.

"SUBURBAN URBANISM" IN INTERIOR DESIGN, VOL. 62, NO. 5, MAY 1999, PP. 292–299.

FILLER, MARTIN, "TWO PART HARMONY" IN HOUSE BEAUTIFUL, FEBRUARY 1999, PP. 96–101.

"RELATIVE MERITS" IN WALLPAPER, FEBRUARY 1999, P. 72.

ZEVON, SUSAN, "PUSHING THE DIGITAL ENVELOPE" IN HOUSE BEAUTIFUL: HOUSES OF THE NEXT MILLENNIUM SERIES, OCTOBER 1998, PP. 66–70.

FRANKEL, ELENA, "MAKING A SPEC HOUSE SPECIAL" IN ARCHITECTURAL RECORD, RECORD HOUSES, APRIL 1998, PP. 68–75.

BERNSTEIN, FRED, "COMFORTS OF MODERN", EDITED BY LINDA O'KEEFE, IN METROPOLITAN HOME, SEPTEMBER/OCTOBER 1997, PP. 132–141.

JACOBS, KARRIE, "SUB-MINIMAL MESSAGE" NEW YORK, FEBRUARY 24, 1997.

BIERMAN, LINDSAY, "SISTER ACT," ED. ELIZABETH SVERBEYEFF BYRON, ELLE DECOR, OCTOBER/NOVEMBER 1995, PP. 268–273.

MERKEL, JAYNE, "REACHING OUT" IN OCULUS, THE AMERICA INSTITUTE OF ARCHITECTS, V57, N9, MAY 1995, PP. 10–11.

PEARSON, CLIFFORD A, "CANADIAN AU PAIR", ARCHITECTURAL RECORD: RECORD HOUSES, APRIL 1995, PP. 96–101.

"THE DIGITAL HABITAT" IN HARPER'S BAZAAR, SEPTEMBER 1995, PP. 346–352.

RUSSEL, BEVERLY, "40 UNDER 40" IN INTERIORS, SEPTEMBER 1995, P. 68.

"CINCINNATI EXHIBITION OF DREAM HOUSES" IN ARCHITECTURE, JANUARY 1994, PP. 27–29.

FILLER, MARTIN, "USER FRIENDLY" IN HOUSE BEAUTIFUL, NOVEMBER 1994, PP. 114–117.

LOUKIN, ANDREA, "HARIRI & HARIRI" IN INTERIOR DESIGN, MARCH 1994, PP. 8–11.

LOUKIN, ANDREA, "HARIRI & HARIRI" IN INTERIOR DESIGN, JULY 1994, PP. 101–103, 148–149.

"JSM MUSIC STUDIOS", ENVIRONMENTS I.D. AWARD, IN I.D., JULY/AUGUST 1993, P. 139.

FRAMPTON, KENNETH, "CRITICISM: ON THE WORK OF HARIRI & HARIRI" IN A+U, JULY 1993, PP. 81–130.

PEARSON, CLIFFORD A., "SUM OF ITS PARTS" IN ARCHITECTURAL RECORD: RECORD HOUSES, APRIL 1993, PP. 76–83.

HAMILTON, WILLIAM L., "CRITIC'S CHOICE" METROPOLITAN HOME, JANUARY/FEBRUARY 1993, PP. 20–23.

TONKINSON, CAROLE, "THE GREATFUL BED" IN ELLE DECOR, APRIL/MAY 1993, P. 64.

"KASH VILLA" IN GA HOUSES 34, PROJECT 1992, PP. 31–33.

"GORMAN RESIDENCE" IN GA HOUSES 31, PROJECT 1991, PP. 94–95.

FREIMAN, ZIVA, "YOUNG ARCHITECTS" IN PA, JULY 1990, PP. 64–65.

GEIBEL, VICTORIA, "MATERIAL WITNESS" IN ARCHITECTURE, JUNE 1990, PP. 64–67.

IOVINE, JULIE V., "SIBLING REVELRY" IN METROPOLITAN HOME, AUGUST 1990, PP. 138–140.

HALL, JOHN, "SISTERS IN THE ASCENDANT" THE WORLD OF INTERIORS, DECEMBER 1989, PP. 44–47.

GANDEE, CHARLES, "THE YOUNG CONTENDERS" IN HG, AUGUST 1988, PP. 86–92.

"DMZ" STOREFRONT FOR ART & ARCHITECTURE EXHIBITION CATALOGUE, FRONT 3, NOVEMBER 1988, P. 60.

STEPHENS, SUZANNE, "TO THE LIGHTHOUSE CREATIVELY" IN THE NEW YORK TIMES, NOVEMBER 24, 1988, P. C3.

AWARDS

ELECTROLUX KITCHEN, DESIGN COMPETITION, THIRD PLACE 2009

INTERIOR DESIGN, BEST OF YEAR AWARD, 2008

NEW YORK SPACES MAGAZINE – TOP 50, 2008

NEW YORK HOME MAGAZINE – TOP 50, 2007

WOMEN IN DESIGN AWARD, 2006

STERNBRAUEREI SALZBURG, COMPETITION, FIRST PRIZE WINNER 2006

DESIGN HALL OF FAME, INTERIOR DESIGN MAGAZINE, ARCHITECTURE AWARD 2005

THE AMERICAN ACADEMY OF ARTS AND LETTERS, ACADEMY AWARDS IN ARCHITECTURE, 2005

HOSPITALITY DESIGN AWARD, 2005, JUAN VALDEZ FLAGSHIP CAFÉ NYC

THE AD 100 – THE WORLD'S TOP DESIGNERS AND ARCHITECTS, AWARD 2004

ST. MARK'S COPTIC CANADIAN VILLAGE, COMPETITION FINALIST 2004

DESIGNING THE HIGH LINE, IDEAS COMPETITION, HONORABLE MENTION 2003

THE CITY'S 100 BEST ARCHITECTS, NEW YORK MAGAZINE, 2002

SAATCHI & SAATCHI AWARD, FINALST FOR INNOVATION AND COMMUNICATION, 2000

40 UNDER 40, AWARD 1996

ARCHITECTURAL RECORD, RECORD HOUSES, AWARD 1995, BARRY'S BAY COTTAGE

THE ARCHITECTURAL LEAGUE OF NEW YORK, EMERGING VOICE, AWARD 1995

IX BIENAL PANAMERICANA DE ARQUITECTURA, AWARD 1994, CASA GORMAN

ID ANNUAL DESIGN, ENVIRONMENTS AWARD 1993, JSM MUSIC STUDIOS

BUILDER'S CHOICE, GRAND DESIGN AWARD 1993, NEW CANAAN HOUSE

ARCHITECTURAL RECORD, RECORD HOUSES, AWARD 1993, NEW CANAAN HOUSE

PROGRESSIVE ARCHITECTURE, YOUNG ARCHITECTS, AWARD 1990

THE ARCHITECTURAL LEAGUE OF NEW YORK, YOUNG ARCHITECTS FORUM, AWARD 1990

EXHIBITIONS

2006

MUSÉE DES ARTS ET MÉTIERS, PARIS, FRANCE
BÉTONS: ÉTONNEZ-VOUS!
"THE MUSEUM OF 21ST CENTURY"

2005

PRATT MANHATTAN GALLERY, NEW YORK, NY, USA
RECORD HOUSES
"NEW CANAAN HOUSE"

THE AMERICAN ACADEMY OF ARTS AND LETTERS, NYC
EXHIBITION OF WORKS BY NEWLY ELECTED
MEMBERS AND RECIPIENTS OF HONORS AND AWARDS

SEAPORT WORLD TRADE CENTER, BOSTON, MA
RECORD HOUSES
"NEW CANAAN HOUSE"

TRIENNALE DI MILANO, MILANO, ITALY
DRESSING OURSELVES
"DIGITAL GEAR"

2004

NATIONAL BUILDING MUSEUM, WASHINGTON, D.C.
LIQUID STONE: NEW ARCHITECTURE IN CONCRETE
"THE MUSEUM OF 21ST CENTURY"

2003

GRAND CENTRAL TERMINAL, NEW YORK, NY
DESIGNING THE HIGH LINE

"HIGH LINE COMMUNITY – OLYMPIC VILLAGE 2012"
DANSK ARKITEKTUR CENTER, COPENHAGEN, DENMARK
FUTURES 2 COME
"THE CINE"

DEUTSCHES ARKITEKTUR MUSEUM
FRANKFURT, GERMANY

A NEW WORLD TRADE CENTER: DESIGN PROPOSALS
"THE WEEPING TOWERS"

GALERIA FERRAN CANO, MALLORCA, SPAIN
I LOVE NEW YORK
"THE WEEPING TOWERS"

2002

CUBE CENTRE, MANCHESTER, U.K
A NEW WORLD TRADE CENTER: DESIGN PROPOSALS
"THE WEEPING TOWERS"

GALERIA FERRAN CANO, BARCELONA, SPAIN
I LOVE NEW YORK
"THE WEEPING TOWERS"

8TH BIENNALE OF ARCHITECTURE IN VENICE, ITALY
A NEW WORLD TRADE CENTER: DESIGN PROPOSALS
"THE WEEPING TOWERS"

NATIONAL BUILDING MUSEUM, WASHINGTON, DC
A NEW WORLD TRADE CENTER: DESIGN PROPOSALS
"THE WEEPING TOWERS"

MAX PROTETCH GALLERY, NEW YORK, NY, USA
A NEW WORLD TRADE CENTER: DESIGN PROPOSALS
"THE WEEPING TOWERS"

2001

MUSEU D'ART CONTEMPORANI DE BARCELONA
BARCELONA, SPAIN
BARCELONA ART REPORT 2001 TRIENNIAL
"THE DIGITAL—HOUSE"

2000

ARMAND HAMMER MUSEUM AT UCLA
LOS ANGELES, CA
THE UN-PRIVATE HOUSE
"THE DIGITAL—HOUSE"

THE WALKER ART CENTER, MINNEAPOLIS
THE UN—PRIVATE HOUSE
"THE DIGITAL—HOUSE"

AUSTRIAN MUSEUM OF APPLIED ARTS
VIENNA, AUSTRIA
THE UN-PRIVATE HOUSE
"THE DIGITAL—HOUSE"

SCI-ARC, LOS ANGELES, CA
2ND INTERNATIONAL ARCHITECTURAL EXHIBIT
& AUCTION, MARCH 2000
"THE DIGITAL—HOUSE"

ARCHITEKTUR SOMMER HAMBURG 2000
HAMBURG, GERMANY
WOMEN AND XTENDED VISIONS
"CINE— EXPERIMENTAL FILM CENTER"

BERKELEY ART MUSEUM, BERKELEY, CA
2X2 EXHIBIT
"CINE & GREENWICH HOUSE"

1999

MAX PROTETCH GALLERY, NEW YORK, NY
FUTURES TO COME: SPONSORED BY
ARCHITECTURAL RECORD
"CINE-EXPERIMENTAL FILM CENTER"

GLASGOW 1999, GLASGOW, UK
DIRECTOR: DEYAN SUDJIC
CURATOR: TULGA BEYERLE
"THE DIGITAL—HOUSE"

THE MUSEUM OF MODERN ART, NEW YORK, NY
THE UN-PRIVATE HOUSE, CURATOR: TERENCE RILEY
"THE DIGITAL—HOUSE"

1996

ROBERT LEHMAN GALLERY
@ URBAN GLASS CENTER, BROOKLYN, NY
"HOUSE FOR THE NEXT MILLENNIUM"

1995

AIA — BALTIMORE
(SIX HOUSES)

1994

THE SECOND PARISH ART MUSEUM
SOUTH HAMPTON, NY
DESIGN BIENNIAL: MIRRORS
"WHAT ARE YOU LOOKING FOR"

D&D BUILDING, NYC
FANTASY CHAIR EXHIBIT
"ON THE ROAD, CHAIR FOR THE HOMELESS"

1993

UNIVERSITY OF HOUSTON, HOUSTON, TX
CITY, ROOM, GARDEN
"URBAN GARDEN"

TEXAS A+M UNIVERSITY, COLLEGE STATION, TX
CITY, ROOM, GARDEN
"URBAN GARDEN"

SCI — ARC, LOS ANGELES, CA
INTERNATIONAL ARCHITECTURAL EXHIBITION AND
SALE (SCHOLARSHIP FUND RAISER)
"KASH VILLA PERSPECTIVE VIEW"

THE CONTEMPORARY ARTS CENTER, CINCINNATI, OH
THE ARCHITECT'S DREAM: HOUSES FOR THE NEXT
MILLENNIUM
"THE NEXT HOUSE"

CORNELL UNIVERSITY, ITHACA, NY
FEMALE CONSTRUCT
"SELECTED PROJECTS"

RICHARD ANDERSON GALLERY, NYC
CURATED BY NANCY SPIRO
" IT IS A MATTER OF FORCE. TENSION ...
COMPRESSION."

1991

KENT STATE UNIVERSITY, KENT, OH
HARIRI & HARIRI CATHARSIS
"RECENT WORK"

1990

THE ARCHITECTURAL LEAGUE OF NEW YORK, NYC
YOUNG ARCHITECTS FORUM 1990
"SELECTED WORK"

1988

PRINCETON UNIVERSITY, PRINCETON , NJ
SELECTED WORK

PARSONS SCHOOL OF DESIGN, NYC
BEARINGS: FACULTY ARCHITECTURE IN
NORTH AMERICA
SELECTED WORK

STOREFRONT FOR ART AND ARCHITECTURE, NYC
PROJECT DMZ, THEORETICAL WORK

LIGHTHOUSE DONATION TO LIGHTHOUSE
DEVELOPMENT CENTER
AUCTION AT TIFFANY & CO. EXHIBITION & PREVIEW
AT D & D BUILDING, NYC

1987

ALLIANCE IN THE PARK, AN OUTDOOR/ INDOOR
EXHIBITION OF COLLABORATIVE WORKS
PHILADELPHIA, PA

MILAN TRIENNALE, URBAN DESIGN EXHIBITION, ITALY
COLLABORATION WITH STEVEN HOLL ARCHITECT, NYC

1986

EQUILIBRIUM PROJECT
VIA NEW YORK
ARCHITECTURAL EXHIBITION IN MEXICO CITY
OTHER PARTICIPANTS: ZAHA HADID, REM
KOOLHAAS, STEVEN HOLL, LEBBEUS WOODS,
GIULIANO FIORENZOLI, ANDREW MCNAIR

ACKNOWLEDGMENTS

With each book I hope to be able to acknowledge and thank people who have inspired, encouraged, supported, built, photographed, and commissioned our projects and buildings. To begin with, this book would have not been possible without the commitment of Alessina Brooks, Paul Latham, Beth Browne, and The Images Publishing Group. I am grateful for their enthusiasm, patience, advice, and willingness to make this book a reality.

Claudia Brandenburg *again* brought her remarkable skill and imagination to the design of our second book together. I am thankful to her for being brilliant, original, and a great partner, making the long process of creating this book such a pleasure. I am also grateful to my friend and publicist Chris Northrup, my team Bieinna Ham and Markus Randler for their tireless effort in putting the material of this book together.

Architecture is impossible without the drive, dedication, and will to continue in spite of all hardship and disappointments. Many interns, designers, and associates have put their minds and hearts into the projects selected for this book. I am thankful to all of them as their dedication, talent, hard work, and love of architecture make them a vitally important part of Hariri & Hariri – Architecture.

We are fortunate to have many old and new friends, patrons, and mentors. I would like to thank them all. I am especially grateful to H.I.M. Empress Farah Pahlavi, Nadja Swarovski, Ernst Scholdan, Alan Webber, Richard Meier, Layla Diba, Leila Taghinia Milani Heller, Iran Issa Khan, Michele Oka Doner, Maryam Seyhoun, Tui Pranich, Lucilo Pena, Kambiz and Nazgol Shahbazi, and all our clients for their longstanding support of our work. They have each inspired, educated, and helped us grow during the past 25 years.

Architecture is not possible without a great team of designers, consulting engineers, contractors, craftsmen, artisans, construction managers, and those who trust our decisions and we trust theirs. We are thankful to you all.

I am extremely grateful to the photographers who have worked with me over many long hours to capture the essence of our work so artfully. In particular, I would like to thank my friend, photographer extraordinaire Paul Warchol for his artistic point of view and always showing me another angle from which to see my own work.

My final thanks are to my sister, partner, and best friend Mojgan Hariri with whom I grew up to be who I am and without whom there would be no Hariri & Hariri – Architecture, thanks for all that you've shared with me and taught me. To my parents Karim and Behjat Hariri, our family and friends for their generous support during the best and worst of times and for never losing confidence in our vision.

And to my partner-in-life, soul mate, and patron, Bahman Kia you are my treasure in life, my center, and refuge. To my two precious daughters Iman and Ava this book means nothing without you. Thank you for allowing me to work long hours away from you. You are my "Voice" and "Faith" in life and this book is for you.